How Not to be just another freelancer

Kaylee White

HOW NOT TO BE JUST ANOTHER FREELANCER

Copyright © 2019 by Kaylee White.

All rights reserved. Printed in the United States of America. No part of this book may be used or reproduced in any manner whatsoever without written permission except in the case of brief quotations em- bodied in critical articles or reviews.

For information contact :
Kaylee White
authorknj@gmail.com
http://www.kayleewrites.com

Cover Design by J.M. Ivie
Book Formatting by Derek Murphy @Creativindie
ISBN: 9781729308493

First Edition: February 2019

10 9 8 7 6 5 4 3 2 1

SIGN UP FOR THE MONTHLY NEWSLETTER

TO RECEIVE SPECIAL OFFERS, GIVEAWAYS, DISCOUNTS, BONUS CONTENT, UPDATES FROM THE AUTHOR, INFO ON NEW RELEASE AND MORE:

WWW.KAYLEEWRITES.COM

Dedication

To my fiancé, Russell Johnston.

Thank you for pushing me to not only turn this into a book, but to pursue my passions every single day. And for making me get out of the house every once in awhile so I don't go crazy.

How Not to be Just Another Freelancer

Kaylee White

CONTENTS

WHY BECOME A FREELANCER 1

FREELANCER VS. BUSINESS OWNER 7

HOW TO EXPERIENCE YOUR PASSION..12

GETTING ORGANIZED 18

TOOLS AND SOFTWARE..29

EMAIL MANAGEMENT..39

WORKFLOWS AND SYSTEMS 49

BUDGETING FOR THE BROKE ENTREPRENEUR 59

GOALS & THE MILLION WAYS TO MAKE THEM 73

BUILDING A CRM..85

WEBSITES...97

STYLE YOUR COPY TO IMPROVE YOUR BRAND 117

MARKETING YOUR SERVICES 124

CONTENT STRATEGY...141

BLOGS 152

NEWSLETTERS AND SOCIAL MEDIA..162

EBOOKS, VIDEOS, AND OTHER UPGRADES...................................176

CONTENT HOARDERS ANONYMOUS...184

MY OVERWHELM KIT 196

BUILDING YOUR TEAM 203

COLD PITCHING VS. JOB BOARDS...209

MANAGING CLIENTS..215

PLANNING THE EVENT OF A LIFETIME..226

MINDSET..233

HOW NOT TO BE JUST ANOTHER FREELANCER 243

KAYLEE WHITE

Why Become a Freelancer

Chapter One

THE WORLD IS UNPREDICTABLE. One day, you have an amazing job with benefits and the next, you're getting fired from a position you've held for more than a decade with no idea what to do next. There's no guarantee anymore. Not only are people scared - they're confused. What are they supposed to do? They have bills to pay and a family to support. They have dreams they want to fund, vacations they want to take, and causes they'd like to support. They don't have time or the ability to have uncertainty in their life. They have responsibilities.

To understand why I believe freelancing is steadier than a full time job, check out Melissa's article, "Why Freelancing Has More Job Security Than a 9-5." I linked the article in a resource center for you. There are tons of resources you have access to. You can find everything on my website at www.kayleewrites.com/hnaf.

Becoming a freelancer gives people the chance to determine their own future. This isn't to say freelancing is easy or even a sure thing. It's going to be a ton of work and it will probably be one of the hardest things you attempt. However, being a freelancer means your future is in your hands. It's all up to you. You get to design your life the way you want. You aren't dependent on anyone else.

This book was something I needed to write. I had so much to say about why freelancing is such a great path for people to take and how they can actually take this path using strategies and methods to become successful. You don't want to be just another freelancer. You want to make something you can be proud of and support your family. You want to be taken seriously. It's all about making your dreams come true and making sure you aren't seen as just another freelancer by potential clients.

My focus wasn't on finding another job to pay me peanuts or stress me out. It was on building relationships, growing my brand, and becoming the type of business owner I always wanted to be. Everything I ever did was to build a business I could be proud of. I didn't know how to make that a reality, so I blindly went into it.

I started my first business in 2013, my junior year of college. I spent a ton of time building the perfect brand and working on perfecting my business method. It was a brownie delivery service for college kids called Brain-Dead Brownies. I poured hundreds of dollars into this business. I spent months perfecting the brownie making methods and working on creating the perfect website and so much more. I didn't do any marketing or try to build a group of followers. I didn't build any relationships. I had no plan when it came to figuring out how the delivery part of the business would work. You can imagine how shocked I was when this business failed utterly.

It's 2018 as I'm writing this and we BARELY paid off the debt from that business. I jumped blindly, not thinking about the consequences or attempting to go about it in a strategic way. I didn't think about how the business would work. This book is here to help you avoid the same mistake I made. It's here to give you the guidance you need to become the freelancer, business owner, entrepreneur of your dreams.

To be able to do that, you need to use this book to its full potential. Take notes in the margins. Add notes to your business notebook. Skip the chapters you don't need. Reread the chapters you need extra help with. Let me know if you have any questions. Work with other people who have read this book and complete the action tasks together. If you start to get overwhelmed with everything we go over, come back to this section. Reread this and know that none of this needs to happen all at once. Take your time. Use the resources you have at your disposal.

You'll find a worksheet in the resource center to help you come up with a realistic timeline to work off of. Don't panic. You can do this. I believe in you. I believe in your skills and abilities. Take it one step at a time and keep going. Even when you have no clients, even when you have horrible clients, even when you have no idea how you're going to make this work. Keep going. I know you want more out of life and you deserve it. Go out and make it happen. Nobody else is going to make this happen for you. You have to do this yourself. You got this!

Freelancer vs. Business Owner

Chapter Two

BEING A FREELANCER CARRIES a lot of stigma. For some people, they feel ashamed. They don't want to tell anyone what they're trying to do. If I'm being honest, I love being a freelancer. I have a very different take on how to be a freelancer and a successful one at that. Since I think of freelancing differently, I also think about being a business owner in a different way. The difference between being a freelancer or a business owner isn't vast.

It can be hard to keep the two separate. Experts seem to always be arguing over what the differences are.

My definition for a business owner is a combination of Melyssa's definition and the definition Jenny Beres and Alexandra Grizinski, the founders of the Six-Figure Freelancer Community, created. A business owner is someone who takes on risk in their business. It's someone who focuses on building reoccurring relationships with clients and building a business around a brand, whether it's themselves or something else. It's where someone is focused on building a platform where they do regular projects or work with the same clients over and over, while also bringing in more clients.

Being a freelancer means you're hired to work for different companies on different assignments. This means you don't typically work with the same businesses or clients on a regular basis. You work on everything under your own name. You don't focus on building a relationship, but rather on getting paid for this one project. You do one job and move on to another client with another project. You focus on finding new clients all the time because you never stick with the same clients for long. You finish a project and move on. You don't have any recurring clients or projects.

This isn't an obvious difference. This isn't a hard

and fast definition either. Someone could consider themselves a business owner when what they are really doing is freelancing. Someone could label themselves a freelancer when they are a business owner. There are no rules to what one calls themselves, nor is there any stagnant definition for what either of these terms mean.

Every freelancer wants a job. They are willing to cut their prices, offer more for less, and basically diminish their value and worth to get a job. Like I said, they are focused on the money and on getting the job. Most freelancers will accept "exposure" as payment and think it will do something for them and their business. That's not you. You know better. Your value and self-worth aren't dependent on getting hired for a job which will only result in peanut pay and several break-downs. You don't want exposure or even experience. You have enough of both of those. You have valuable skills worth something. You know you can do better. So why don't you?

Don't cut your prices. Establish a rate and stick with it or establish a system for creating rates for each project based on the amount of work, not on hours or exposure. Create a system for what to do when someone asks you for work. Take each person you come into contact with and add them into a Customer Relationship

Management (CRM) tool. Follow up with previous clients and ask if they need anything. Create a marketing plan that gives you a ton of leads and increases traffic to your website. Even if you call yourself a freelancer, taking these actions will help streamline your customer experience and gain you more repeat customers.

You know I utterly failed in my first business. I never let that stop me. I've spent the last five years gaining experience and learning as much as I can about how to build an online business. After the brownie business, I started a blog called Bright Colors Happy Things. I started and restarted that blog about four times. I went on to becoming a marketing strategist who offered marketing strategy plans for clients. I also built a business offering social media strategy. Then, I started copywriting. My mom suggested I offer writing as a business and the light bulb clicked. I've been writing ever since. I "officially" started my copywriting business in September 2016 so it's been a fun two year journey so far. I can't wait to see where I am in the next five years!

Remember the path to accomplishing your dreams is not a straight one. Starting to think of your freelance work like a business will help bring you more clientele. More clientele means more income. More income means more freedom. You're a business owner, whether you want the title or not. Stop killing yourself on job boards and start taking a vested interest in your work. Build a relationship with your clients and start working on multiple projects.

As Jenny and Alex always say, "This is not a gift. They are not doing you a favor. It is an exchange of mutual beneficial value, energy, and services." You should get paid what you're worth and your clients should get work that's worth what they paid.

How to Experience Your Passion

Chapter Three

You may be the type of freelancer who is freelancing because it's extra money and while you don't want it to be your full-time career, you're enjoying doing it now. You may be the type of freelancer who has an intense passion for what you do and you decided to make a business out of it. Either way, society is clamoring for you to figure out what you're passionate about and to stick to that one thing. This can be hard, especially if you're someone like me.

I've never had a hobby or thing I was truly, deeply passionate about. I loved doing a lot of things. I wanted to be in marketing, become an expert in Ancient Egypt, become an American Sign Language interpreter, publish some books, be a business owner, work in social media, help take care of animals, be a mom, be a professional motivational speaker, become a teacher, professionally organize people, and become an event planner. Seriously, the amount of things I've wanted to be in my life grows every time my attention changes. Which doesn't help when my attention span is about as long as a goldfish's.

Some people truly know what they want to be from the time they were able to talk. They chose their path back then and did everything in their power to get to that point. They had intense and fierce passion for their chosen path. They didn't let anything get in their way. This is the same attitude you have to take in the business world. Passion is the main ingredient for business success. It doesn't matter if you want this to become a full-time job or stay a side job, you need to be passionate about it.

When you are trying to live a full life, go do something. You're never going to find your passion if you're moping in your room staring at a screen of nothing. Try something you enjoy. Create experiences. Take action towards finding what you're passionate about. This isn't the time to sit back and hope something hits you in the head with a brilliant idea. You have to go out and "find" your passion. That's why they call it finding your passion and not waiting for your passion to hit you upside the head.

All this to say, I actually believe having a passion is overrated. We place way too much emphasis on finding the one thing we want to do for the rest of our lives. There is no way you are only passionate about one single thing in your entire life. You may have one passion in life, but it's probably not the only thing in your life. You probably love a few other things you're passionate about. It's something you do because it interests you and you want to get more involved with it. You're doing it because you love it and you enjoy it. This is the type of passion I believe everyone should find.

The only way you'll be able to actually find your passion is to go out and find it. Try hobbies, participate in events, do things you enjoy - for the sole purpose of doing them. Do something. It doesn't matter what. Create experiences. Take time to try new things. Sign up for new classes. Rekindle your love for an old hobby. Your passion isn't something you should stop searching for, even if you've found it. It's an ongoing, ever-changing part of your life and you need to focus on finding each and every passion your heart longs for.

Knowing the difference between a passion and a hobby is crucial to figuring out what is yours. Jenika from Psychology for Photographers actually has my favorite definition of the two. She says a hobby is "a pursuit outside one's regular occupation engaged in especially for relaxation." She goes on to explain in older English, a passion meant suffering and therefore is something you are overwhelmingly devoted to, and some might say, obsessed with. It's something you're willing to suffer through to keep doing. A hobby is something you're doing because it's fun. If there is too much suffering associated with it, you wouldn't mind giving up and moving on to something else. You wouldn't put too much effort into dealing with obstacles which occur.

I've downloaded worksheets, watched hundreds of videos, and read a bunch of books trying to figure out what my passion is. At the end of the day, I only found out what I was passion about by doing something. I started writing and working towards things I enjoyed doing, trying to see which one I was willing to endure suffering for. When I say suffer, I don't mean physical pain - although, depending on your passion, some may be involved. I mean when you incur an obstacle which gives you a hard time while you're trying to enjoy your passion. This could mean you don't have the right supplies or the necessary funds. It could mean you have no idea how to actually do your hobby. The "suffering" can be small.

The answer to my passion wasn't some profound thing. It was literally figuring out what I love. I grew up loving reading. I would get caught by my parents with a book and a flashlight under my blanket at 2 am in the morning, many times. Something so simple and natural to me became the thing I was most passionate about. The problem to learning what I was passionate about is I thought it had to be something big. I thought I had to have a light bulb moment to find what it was.

To combat my confusion in figuring out all of my hobbies, I crafted a personal statement. I hoped this statement would help me focus my energy and get me to understand what I was trying to accomplish in my life. With the help from a few articles from Boho Berry and the Mission Statement Builder from Franklin Covey, all linked in our resource center, I created one.

HOW NOT TO BE JUST ANOTHER FREELANCER

For those of you interested, my mission statement is:

to be transparent, relatable, and consistent in an effort to inspire, educate, and encourage others; to create space that encourages love, compassion, and a high value of kindness

Getting Organized

Chapter Four

GETTING STARTED AS A freelancer is a big deal. Between setting up all of the accounts, figuring out how to find clients, understanding how a business works, and so much more, it's no wonder you're feeling overwhelmed. I know I felt exactly the same way! The best way to manage your feeling of overwhelm is to get organized. The problem comes in that even that step can be overwhelming! You have to choose where to put everything and how to organize it. Between all the different types of notebooks and all the online software available, there really can be too many options. It can seriously cause you to freeze. That's not what we're going to do. You've got the skills and the right tools. We're going to rock this.

When you find yourself unable to move forward, the best course of action is to stop trying to move. Take a step back (okay, so there's a little bit of movement) and really think over everything you've got going on. If you're like me, you are always in a different place when you work. You're never really in the same place and you never know when you'll be able to work on your business. For that reason, I organize my work mostly online. I use two project management software tools, Asana and Trello, to organize my life, finances, and business. For any notes I need to take, I have one business notebook I treat like a bullet journal and keep track of everything there.

If you are always working in the same place or want to work on your business during a designated time in a specific place, you may not need as much as I do to keep track of everything. Maybe you use a physical planner and one project management software tool in connection with each other. Maybe you don't want to learn a new software and decide to organize everything in spreadsheets housed in Google Docs and Google

Calendar. This is perfectly acceptable!

The biggest piece of advice I can offer is to figure out how you work best. Do you get distracted easily? It's probably not a good idea to be online all the time then. Are you a visual person? Physical notebooks or Trello are the best options. Figure out how you work and organize based on that.

I work best and understand material more when I hand write my notes. Knowing this, my first steps to getting organized included setting up my business notebook, clearing out my inbox, clearing out my paperwork, and setting up my lists in Asana and Trello.

My business notebook was simple to set up. I decided I wanted to keep all of my notes here. This notebook is going to be used to house all of my client phone calls, any webinars, videos, or courses I took or wanted to take notes on, and all of the projects I started. It goes everywhere with me.

The next thing to do was clear out my inbox. This was so I could keep my focus on building my business and not managing the incoming junk emails. I went through and cleared all of my emails - I have like five of them. We'll talk about email management later, but for now, all you need to know is I took a day and deleted pretty much everything. If I hadn't read an email from someone's newsletter list for the last three months, I was probably never going to read it so it got deleted and I unsubscribed.

My next task was to get my paperwork cleared out. I spent the better part of a year downloading and hoarding other people's content. I go deeper into the fun part of my life later, just know I had four 3" binders FULL of downloads, courses, PDF's, and so much more, just waiting for me to fill them out.

I was overwhelmed and ridden with guilt trying to keep up with filling out all of the documents I kept downloading. It kept me stuck in the same place I was in for over a year. I ended up throwing away everything. I wiped my slate clean. I know this seems hard, but there's nothing in those downloads you don't already know.

My last step was to get my Asana and Trello boards set up. Trello is my main project management software. I have a board where I house all of my ideas for my YouTube Channel videos, which step they're on, and if I have any notes about them. I have a board where I house all of my goals for each month, as well as my goals for the year. They are broken down into smaller tasks I need to complete in order to accomplish my overall goal. I have a board for my clients, with a list of all their projects, what they're worth, what step they're on, and when they're due.

My Asana account houses lists which need a bit more organizing in terms of structure. My publishing plan for this book was housed on there for instance, because I needed to list out the big tasks, list out the sub tasks those big tasks required, and had even more smaller tasks which needed to be accomplished. Asana is great for organizing all of the subtasks a project requires. It also houses all of the template information I need, like my YouTube channel link, any hashtags I use, links to videos and so much more.

I spent quite a bit of time getting all of this stuff organized and set up. Things changed regularly and I continually updated my process until I found out what worked. I still tweak it regularly when I need to refresh my process. My life is less chaotic and I know how to process all of the information I receive. I know where it goes, how to interact with it, and what to do with it once it is in place. Taking a step back and doing these seemingly small tasks can help create a peace of mind and a sense of professionalism in a matter of hours. This can calm any anxiety or overwhelm and make you a better business owner.

Once you've taken time to find out how you're going to organize information, clear out any old information cluttering your mind, and figure out how you work best. You want to start off by making a business email. I know - another email account?! Trust me when I say it's necessary. This email is the foundation of your business. You don't want to miss out on a $5,000 retainer with a client because you skimmed through and missed it in-between an email for free goat's milk and your grandma asking how you work email.

All of your accounts will be connected to this email. All perspective and current clients will see it. Don't skimp on this. Gmail for Work is $5 a month for an email with your own domain name. You instantly look more professional. If you aren't willing to invest $5 a month, are you sure you're committed to your success?

DISCLAIMER: I'm assuming you've already decided on your business name, even if it's your own name, and have purchased your domain name.

Once you've secured your email, you can set up the bare bones of your social media profiles. Pick out your username, add a profil photo, and a biography written. They should all be similar.

Once your email and social media are set up, you should focus on creating samples of your work. These samples can be housed on your website or sent directly to potential clients. I know a lot of you will want to put it on a website, because that's what you think you should be doing. The truth is, you don't need a website. You can get by without having one. Try it for awhile. If you find it doesn't work for you, then create a website and house your samples on there.

Your focus needs to be on creating samples of the work you want to be doing. Use existing samples you have, make up fake companies and create a sample for them, or create a sample for an established company you love to showcase the work you would love to produce. **A warning:** do not send this sample to the established company. You'll look incredibly unprofessional. Use this sample purely as a sample. Include a line like "Here's what I would produce for SUCH-AND-SUCH, I think something like this would work for you and your goals."

Whether you set up a website or not, take the time to set up a Customer Relationship Management (CRM) tool. The basics of this is to get all of your contacts into the tool and use it for everything. Keep all information you gather about clients, potential clients, partners, vendors, mentors, everyone goes in here. This way when you want to reach out and build a relationship up, you know exactly who to reach out to and what you're going to say. Plus, you never have to ask someone to "refresh your memory" on a conversation you guys had. It's all written down and ready for you to skim over and refresh yourself. You look incredibly professional and impress the other person when you remember details of past conversations.

Organizing your business is a big job. Use your organization to maintain your professional appearance, keep you from going crazy, and move your business forward. I spent a good month or so learning exactly what I needed, how I wanted to organize it, and putting workflows and procedures in place. Now, anytime a client calls me or I have someone I need to onboard into my business, I know exactly what to do and where to put all of the information. I know exactly what the next step is and how to communicate to the person I'm working with.

This is not the time to be lazy. Organizing isn't meant to be a task you half-do. Taking the time to put an effort into organizing everything will make the difference between you seeming like an amateur and a professional. Yes, it seems silly, but you having all of their information sorted and stored really does make you seem like you know what you're doing - even if you don't. Even if this is your first ever business, you're terrified, and you have absolutely no idea what you're doing, completing all of these tasks can make you seem like you've been in business for years and this is just a walk in the park.

Tools and Software

Chapter Five

IF YOU WERE INSPIRED by our last chapter and are ready to start organizing, pay attention. I think I'll skip naming all of them. I'm only going to introduce a few of them I use daily and absolutely love. Keep in mind, you don't need to use these. What you need to take away from this chapter is you need to find a software which you enjoy in order to use these tools to keep organized.

The tools I use are simple, cheap, and easy to get started with but do the job I need them to do. I didn't purchase expensive tools for the sake of going with the expensive option. I looked at a ton of different options and went with what worked best for my business. You should do the same. The tools listed below are a great starting point for you to look into; however, you don't need to stick with these if they don't work for you. Feel free to look into others and try different things. These are going to be tools you use each and everyday. You need them to be tools you enjoy using.

The first tool I suggest to everyone getting into freelancing of any type is Gmail. I know we talked about this a bit in the last chapter, and I'm probably going to go over it again a couple more times throughout this book, but it's such an incredible tool! Not only are you able to completely organize all of your incoming and outgoing emails, you're also able to build a YouTube channel, organize and create documents in Google Docs, and have video chats with other people. This is an incredible tool everyone needs to use on a regular basis.

Another tool I use on a regular basis is my accounting software! I currently use Wave Accounting. It's a free accounting software which allows me to process credit cards, send invoices, and keep track of all of the transactions run through my business. I know Quickbooks is also a great software if you're willing to invest in this tool. Right now, it makes sense for my business to be in Wave, but as it continues to grow, I will most likely be moving over to Quickbooks. Remember, there are millions of different software for each tool I mention here. You need to experiment and find the perfect one for you and your business.

Another tool I use each and everyday is a project management system. We discussed Trello and Asana in the last chapter, but there is no perfect project management software. The perfect one is the one you use on a regular basis. While I focus on Trello and Asana, consider Basecamp, Freedcamp, Todoist, Milanote, or even One Note. It needs to be something you can access and use from anywhere. Also, it needs to be one you enjoy using on a regular basis. You'll be in it several times a day.

The next tool you'll find vital is online storage space. It doesn't matter whether you store photographs or documents, you're going to need some place to store information. I use Google Drive as my main source of storage. I also have a free storage account with Dropbox and Evernote so I have more places and room to store documents. I also have a 1TB portable hard drive for my bigger projects and back up copies of my files. Images used for my website, social media, and marketing, the videos I record for my YouTube channel, and all of the contracts and work I do for my clients all need to be stored in these accounts. I need as much room as I can get.

The next tool you'll want to look into is a website host. We'll go in-depth later, but you should know I'm a SquareSpace girl. I absolutely love the functionality of it and the ability to change and update anything I want myself. I have absolutely no technical knowledge, so Wordpress is difficult for me. This is in no way to say Wordpress is worse than SquareSpace. The beautiful websites coming from designers who use Wordpress should be considered near magic. I absolutely love the freedom of Wordpress sites, however, I'm not skilled enough to keep them up to date. I like to change, update, and play around with many different aspects on a website. Know the type of person you are and go from there. There is no one - size fits all. That's why there are so many options.

There are only a couple more tools I want to introduce you to, so pay attention. This next one is literally one of my favorite tools I've ever found: Canva. This is a dumbed down version of Photoshop. You can add text to a photo, create beautiful graphics, and make your brand cohesive with a simple click of a few buttons

- sorry, it's not just one button. There are in fact multiple buttons, but I promise there are a lot less buttons than Photoshop. It's also incredibly easy to learn and use, so you don't have to have a ton of skill to create what you're looking for. This in no way replaces your graphic designer. The skills they have and the amount of work they do will never be able to be emulated with something like Canva. Canva is not meant to replace them, but merely help you keep your cost down on simple things like adding text to an image.

Another tool we've discussed is a Customer Relationship Management (CRM) tool. I've used PipeDrive's CRM, Hubspot's CRM, and Streak CRM. They are all fantastic and beautifully created tools which have helped me at one point or another in my business. The one I currently use is Streak CRM. This is a Gmail Plug-in. I enjoy the workflow of this tool, as it plugs directly into my email account and is able to keep track automatically of all the emails I send out. It's a great tool to use if you don't want to have to work too hard to keep up with your CRM. For now, you need to remember this tool is the lifeline of your business. Set it up and use it well. Use it often.

My last tool isn't exactly a tool. It's a membership platform. I recommend this platform to anyone and everyone who is interested in working in freelancing and wants to learn the tricks of the trade. This platform is where I learned most of my skills and knowledge. It's how I got to be where I am today. This platform is called The Six-Figure Freelancer Academy. It's a monthly membership hosted by Jenny Beres and Alexandra Grizinski. They are also the founders of The Six-Figure Freelancer Community, the Facebook group we talked about in Chapter 2. This is probably one of the most education intense memberships I've ever held and has given the most return on investment (ROI) out of any membership, course, and workshop I've ever seen. If you are interested in this membership at all, check out my resources page.

Now, of course, these aren't the only tools available or maybe even necessary for a business. That being said, I did want to add two bonus tools to check out - CoSchedule and Grum. These are different social media management tools. I LOVE Grum and how simple it is. It's an Instagram management tool. You literally upload the photo, add a caption, type out what you want your first comment to be (hashtags) and schedule when it should be posted. A live person will go in at the appointed time and upload the post for you. This complies with Instagram's Terms of Service in that a live person has to be posting on the platform. I know it's changed a bit in the last year or so and who knows, by the time you're reading this, it may be completely different, but even still Grum is so simple and easy to use I will probably never give it up.

The other tool, CoSchedule, is a fantastic social media management platform. It allows you to actually write and schedule out blog posts, Facebook, Twitter, LinkedIn, and Pinterest posts. It gives you the ability to schedule your Instagram posts and then sends you a reminder to go into the platform and post it. The platform and the beauty of having everything in the same place can't be overlooked. It seriously is so helpful in managing campaigns, launches, and everyday social media strategies. If you need any help with CoSchedule, check out Stephanie Contrad, a productivity expert who specializes in helping overwhelmed people simplify their lives. She has YouTube video walkthroughs on it, all linked on our resource page.

There are many tools a business could need and use. These tools have helped me get to where I am today and they will help me get so much further. It doesn't matter which software you use, only that you use it regularly and you like using it. There will always be another software with better functionality or design.

Don't be tempted to switch because of a pretty logo or webpage. It needs to fit you, your business, your price point, and where you're at.

Email Management

Chapter Six

EVERYONE HAS AN EMAIL account these days. Heck, I am currently managing five of them. All of them are mine and I have to go through all of them at least once a week. Several of them I check once or twice a day. Yes, it's ridiculous. Yes, it's a lot of email accounts to manage, even more to do when I have to start going through and taking action on it all. It can be overwhelming and intense to deal with. Managing all of that information requires a strategy.

I'm betting you're in the same boat. You may have more or less accounts. Heck, you may only have one or two accounts, but you receive hundreds of emails throughout the day. Having a strategy is vital to managing your email, regardless of which situation you're facing. Not having a strategy or plan of attack is going to result with you missing something. An email falls through the cracks, you forget to respond to someone, or you respond to the wrong person and mess up a relationship. Not having a strategy or plan can result in any one of these things happening - or worse.

It's all about creating a workflow. When an email comes in, what do you do with it? How do you handle it? What type of actions do you need to complete? How do you process the emails? What will you do when the email is completed? What will you do with the email when you are waiting on information or someone else before it is complete? Figuring out answers like these can help you create a workflow for tackling all of the work that comes in. These workflows don't have to be complicated or account for every single item which may come into your account. It needs to be broad, simple, and easy to follow.

My email management workflow is super simple. When an email comes in, I obviously start with reading it. Sometimes that's the hardest step when you have 23,000 emails in your account. I can't even have one unread email in my account, but my fiancé has over 10,000 unread emails in the account, but we don't want to speak about that forbidden account. Back to what we were saying - I read the email. Sometimes I only need to look at the sender or the subject line to know its spam or advertisements. I'm able to delete it without ever opening it. If it is an email I need to open and read, I start with some questions to figure out what needs to be done:

- Is the email asking me to do something?
- Does the email give me information about a project or relationship?
- Is the email asking for me to provide more information?
- Do I need this email?
- Is this email important enough to demand some of my attention?

Once I determine what this email is asking, I determine my next course of action. If I don't need the email, I delete it. Right away. I don't let it sit in my inbox, wondering if I'll ever need it or wondering if I should keep a copy, just in case. Nope, it goes right into the trash. I don't want useless emails cluttering up my inbox. I've got enough traffic going through there. I don't need anything else slowing down my workflow. If I can't delete it right away, I figure out what I can do with it.

I'm personally a BIG "If you don't see it, it won't get done" type of person. If I need to complete an action, it needs to be right in front of my face to remind me I need to do it. For all of my email accounts, if I need to take action or follow up on an email, the email stays in my inbox. This way, every time I go into that email account, the email is one of the first things I see, since it's still in there. It irks me to have all of these emails sitting in my inbox.

Pro Tip: *Your goal should be to clear out your inbox on a regular basis. Whether that means emptying it out daily, weekly, or monthly, you should always have a designated time when you go through and empty out your inbox as much as possible. This is when you catch up on all of your categorizing and deleting.*

For my work email, I use the Microsoft Outlook program. I flag and check off every email I complete. If the email doesn't have a checkmark, then I know I haven't completed everything I've needed to for that particular email. Once the email has a check-mark, it gets moved to the appropriate folder. I keep it simple for work. I literally only have three possible folders: Events, Junk, and Students. I handle parking for big events at my job so every email relating to an event, questions about parking, or general customer emails go into this folder.

Any generic HR emails, emails from my boss, emails ordering something, or emails which aren't specifically about events go into this folder. My last email is all about the students. We employ a lot of students and I manage the interviews, hiring, schedules, and any HR issues which may come up with them. All emails they send me, emails concerning them, or emails with scheduling information go, you guessed it, into this folder.

For my freelancing business, I have a few more folders I sort my emails into. In case you forgot, I use Gmail for Work. This means there's no actual "folders" in Gmail, only "labels" which act like folders. An email will get labeled and then archived when it's complete. Then, any time I need to recall that email, I use Gmail's search bar or go into the actual label I created. The labels I created are accounting, clients, general business, leads, and learning. I use these labels loosely, but every email gets put into at least one of these labels.

All invoices, bills, and general financial information goes into my accounting folder. Anything a client sends me, whether for a project or just a question, goes into my client folder. My general business folder is where I house general information. Maybe I worked on a passion project or guest post. This is where I would store those emails. My lead folder is where everyone who asked me a question, inquired about a service, held a conversation with me and I want to nurture into a potential client, or got introduced to me all go. My learning folder is for all of the newsletters I subscribe to, pretending like I'm going to read them.

That's about it for email management. Managing emails isn't hard to do, it just takes work in order to do it. You need to make sure you have a system in place. Systems are literally your best friend (we're going to be talking more about them in the next chapter). Once you have a system and workflow in place, you need to keep on top of it. You can't just put the system in place and expect it to run itself. You need to put the effort in and make the system work. Set up a schedule and figure out when you will make sure you've emptied out your entire inbox. For me, I try at the end of everyday to make sure my inbox is emptied. If not, at least every week it gets cleared completely out.

What works best for me is following my system and taking it one step further. Once I have all of the emails I don't need cleared out and my makeshift to-do list is created, I transfer all of those action items to my actual to-do list. Whether they hit my Trello boards, get placed into my physical calendar/planner, or added to my master to-do list in my business notebook, they are all taken out of my email account and added somewhere that I regularly access throughout the day. The emails stays in my inbox until I complete them, but the actual task items and any details I may need move to my workflow tools. This way I don't have to sit in my email all day. I can focus on actually getting the work done and getting a ton of action items completed.

    This isn't magic and there is no miracle here. It may feel like a miracle needs to happen for you to get through all of the emails in your inbox, but unfortunately, all that needs to happen is a bit of hard work and focus. Even if you have 50,000 emails in one account, you need to go through them all and delete them or get them answered.

    You don't need to spend 30 minutes on one email. If you read the subject, have no idea what it's talking about, and it's not from someone important, delete the email. Get rid of it. You don't need it. For the most part, each email should take you less than a minute. Unless the email actually requires some action on your part, it's either getting deleted or moved to the appropriate folder. This shouldn't be hard. No more wishing or hoping - it's time to get to work.

Pro Tip: *If you've been subscribed to a newsletter or company's sales emails and you haven't opened, much less read an email from them in the last three months, it's time to unsubscribe and delete all of their emails. You haven't read any of their emails. Even if they write a spectacular email and are endorsed by the President of the United States, it needs to go. It's not helping you in any way.*

Workflows and Systems

Chapter Seven

AS A NEW BUSINESS owner, it's so easy to jump into working in the business, finding clients, building a brand, and doing day-to-day tasks. No time to stop and create workflows or systems. Why do you even need them if you only have a few clients? There's always a few clients who are a special circumstance as well who never really fit into a category. Workflows and systems are useless when you're first starting out. You should focus on getting clients and making money, not on creating a workflow you're never going to follow and is useless 90% of the time.

These are the exact thoughts I had when I first started my business. This was the mindset I kept throughout the first two years of trying to run a business. This is a big mistake. Creating workflows and systems helps you avoid becoming overwhelmed. This is the first step you can take to working on your business, instead of in it. Workflows keep your business running smoothly, ensure no information is lost, and keep you from losing your mind. Workflows are literally the backbone of your business. Not incorporating them into your business now is a huge mistake.

A workflow is the sequence of industrial, administrative, or other processes through which a piece of work passes from initiation to completion. Basically, a workflow is something you can follow which has a step-by-step process. It takes you from one side, most of the time frustrated and confused, to the other side, in charge and encouraged to keep going. You can follow the workflow from one end to the other and actually accomplish something. You come out the other side with some type of result.

Workflows not only help you keep your mind and business from running amok, but they help automate so much as well. Automation is important because it lets you scale your business quickly and gives you the opportunity to pass tasks on to either a tool or another person. It grows your income potential without growing your working hours to 80 hours a week. Automation allows you to spend more time with your family, make more money, and enjoy your business again. Automation only occurs when you have a working and useful workflow in place. It only works if you know how to set it up. You can't set anything up if you don't even know how you want it to work. You need a system to understand what kind of workflow you want to put in place. You need a workflow to understand how to automate it.

Creating workflows makes building your team a cinch. Establishing these workflows allows you to bring someone new in, teach them the steps, and then let them run free. Having a clear cut workflow thought out and written down will save any confusion or misunderstanding which may occur. Plus, your team member can't come back and say they didn't know how to do something or what the next step was when you've got the process clearly detailed out.

A workflow and system that's in place and running smoothly saves you so much time and truly grows your business exponentially. Plus, it gives you the illusion of seeming professional. Even if in reality it's sitting in bed working with your pajamas on and Harry Potter in the background, while your fiancé snores his lungs out and your dog is sprawled across the foot of the bed, having the right workflow can make your clients think you've got the big corner office and know exactly what you're doing.

Enough about the benefits of workflows. If you haven't gotten the hint by now, I'm not sure what else to do to convince you. Let's move on to setting up your first workflow.

Start by figuring out which workflows you need to establish. This is your starting point. When you're a freelancer, you're working with clients - duh. Clients mean work is involved, as well as phone calls, emails, and collaboration. We took care of the emails in the last chapter and talked about potential workflows for how to handle an email that comes in. When it comes to talking to a potential client, a workflow here would be immensely useful. First, they need to be put into your customer relationship management tool (CRM). This is where you can get a history created and house the information you want to remember.

Once all of the information is recorded, figure out how you're going to proceed. Do they need to sign a contract? When do they get that contract? How do you get paid? How do you let them know how much they owe you? When do they actually pay you (hint: it's **before** you start the project)? When do you start the work you just got paid for? How do you figure out the particulars regarding the type of work you're doing? Do they need to fill out a questionnaire? When do they get that questionnaire? What do you do with the drafts and final project you create for your client? You need to know how to take them from a potential client to your actual client and beyond. This is what is known as an onboarding workflow.

Now you will probably need a project management workflow. This is a workflow that allows you to manage all of those projects you are getting from all of your different clients. Maybe you chose one of the tools we talked about in Chapter 5 to deal with managing your projects, something like Trello or Asana. No matter what tool you choose, you need a workflow to know how to use it to keep track of everything.

Do you put in every project and if so, which list does it go in? Does it require its own list? Who is responsible for these items? How do you know if the project is being worked on? Where in the project are you right now? Do you know how much further you need to go to complete it? This may seem super overwhelming, but using a project management tool regularly and productively, along with the right workflow, will allow you to manage it all much easier. No longer will your project management tool taunt you with the possibility of order and ease, only to end with unorganization and frustration.

Another workflow you can put together is one for when you and a client part ways after a project. Do you need to send a final invoice? Do they owe you money? Will you send a thank you note or will it be a note of some *other* sort (hint: don't send that one). When do you update your CRM? Do you need to update any paperwork or send any last emails? This all needs to be laid out in a workflow. You don't want a client you parted ways with on bad terms to receive a newsletter email about the lessons you learned from working with them or to get another invoice reminder they don't need.

Having these workflows figured out - and written down - will help you be more focused on what you need to do, know exactly what to do when something in your business changes, and will boost your confidence, abilities, and professionalism. It will make you seem like you've got everything together and you know how to be a business owner. It gives you a step-by-step process for you to follow so when you're freaking out and overwhelmed, you don't have to figure out what to do next. You just take the next step in the process.

Once you've decided which workflows you're going to create, you need to figure out how you're going to actually make them. Whether you spend four days or four hours creating these, you need it to be in a format which makes it easy to understand and follow. If you spend time creating this workflow, and it turns out convoluted and nobody understands it, it's not useful. If you slap it together, nobody is really going to understand or use it when it's needed.

Whether you create a flowchart complete with pictures and arrows or write it out in quick bullet points, you need to communicate your workflow in the clearest and simplest way possible. A fifth grader needs to be able to understand and use this workflow. They should be able to execute every step in this process. The reason being is you don't want your employees or contractors to complain they don't understand? You don't want them to be confused and doing the wrong things. It needs to be incredibly simple. Got it?

Not having created any workflows is a situation you simply can't afford to be in. Aside from ending up having to recreate the wheel every time you encounter a situation and thus wind up doing the same work over and over, you'll also look incredibly unprofessional. You'll flounder, be uncertain, second-guess yourself, not know what the next step should be, and completely come off as an amateur who's in over their head. Put these workflows together and go from amateur to kickass in a matter of seconds.

Budgeting for the Broke Entrepreneur

Chapter Eight

REMEMBER BACK IN THE first chapter how we talked about what being a business owner actually meant? We decided a business owner is someone who takes on financial risk in some way. This can be a scary concept. Everytime I talk about "financial risk," I immediately imagine being stuck in a room with about a dozen stuffy bank guys who are arguing about whether or not my dream is worth funding and if I'm worth investing in. How terrifying is that? I never want someone else to have power over whether my dream comes true or not.

When I talk about "financial risk," I'm talking about the new age definition: any monetary investment you put into your business, no matter how big or small. This includes all of the income you add yourself, any loans you get from friends or parents, and anything you get from sponsors, investors, or the bank. Basically, any money that goes into your business is an investment and you need to keep track of it. Its part of the "risk" you've taken on as a business owner. It's not this big scary thing. It's just part of the process you've decided to take on. You need to understand what it entails and how to deal with it.

Using a budget is good business advice. Not only are you keeping track of everything you spend and can potentially deduct for your taxes, but it helps to know what kind of money you need in order to keep up with all of your business expenses. Having a budget in place helps you run your business when you're living paycheck to paycheck and trying to support your business with your own money. It keeps you from getting into too much debt and dealing with a negative balance while trying to keep the business afloat. A budget is necessary.

HOW NOT TO BE JUST ANOTHER FREELANCER

It is vital.

Alright.

I've convinced you to make a budget. Or you're nodding along, rolling your eyes at me, wishing I'd just move on. Trust me, when we get this setup, you'll feel much better. It'll help keep you organized and focused on what you're trying to accomplish. If you've been in business awhile and have receipts, get them all gathered together. Pull up your bank statements and sharpen your pencils. You're in for a bit of a rough couple of hours. You will need to make sure you know exactly what your current numbers are and how you will hit them every month.

If you are just getting started, you're at a bit of an advantage. You're able to start from scratch. You can tell your budget where to go. You can pick and choose softwares that fit you and your budget completely. You can customize your budget to fit where you want to take your business focus. You're able to sit down and test a bunch of things before you even get started. It's a lot easier to start from scratch then to figure out how to change directions in the middle of everything else you're doing.

Budget time.

First things first, sit down and list out your expenses. If you're just starting out, this list may change, but list all of the expenses you believe you're going to have. For example, the five dollars you spend for Gmail each month? That needs to go on it. The $10 you spend on your domain every year should be added. Keep track of every single penny spent and coming in. This is going to be the basis of your business budget. It's very important you get as accurate numbers as you can so it gives you an accurate representation of what your business looks like.

Your list may look something like this:

CRM	$10	(month)
Gmail	$5	(month)
Website Host	$15	(month)
Pro Membership	$20	(month)
Monthly Budget		$50
Total Yearly Budget	$600	

Seeing this number can seem big, scary, and put on a ton of pressure. It's a big deal to realize you need to be making about $600 a year to keep your business afloat.

You don't even really make a profit off of that money. That's a lot of pressure to put on yourself, especially when you're just starting out! If you've already started your business, you may have been paying for this without even knowing it. It may be the reason why your account has no money at the end of the month. You may be paying for a tool you don't even really use anymore, but are still paying for. Compiling this type of information will help you determine what is vital and what is useless.

Since you've compiled your annual expenses, let's take a look at the potential income you've got coming in this year. This includes products you're going to launch this year. This part isn't even thinking about the income from any clients you may have or sign on throughout the year. Let's look at a big project you've been working on. You've determined you wanted to launch it in the third quarter and since it's your signature product, you determined you wanted to price it fairly decent, as it will be your main offering. How many of these do you need to sell to cover your expenses?

Math time!

Don't make that face. It has to be done. If you need $600

to cover your expenses for the year, plus the $100 you should be saving for your taxes, you need to make at least $700. Let's go a step further. You also know you want to make, at the least, $400 for you to take home. That means you need to make $1,100. This helps you determine your signature product price of $40. When you price your signature product, you determine you will need at least 28 people to purchase this product in order to make your budget work.

28 people - that doesn't seem so bad does it? All of your expenses are paid for the year, plus you took care of some taxes and even got a little profit on top. Your next step is to figure out how to get 28 people to purchase your product. Maybe add a timed bonus (a workbook or other content that is available for a limited time with purchase of your product). Maybe you host a webinar the week before your product goes on sale to promote it. Maybe you team up with another business owner and create a package together. You could even host a giveaway to promote buzz. Whatever you choose to do, you need to have a plan to get the minimum number of customers to purchase your product.

I'm sure this $40 product isn't the only one you're planning to sell this year. Plus, if you get more than 28 people to purchase your product, you end up making more income. For every product you develop and launch, go through the same exercise. If you want to up your income level, you need to figure out how many people you will need to purchase each of your products and at what price. This will give you an idea of how much work you need to do. This gives you an estimate for your annual income.

I want to address all of you who are service-based businesses. You may come back to me with the excuse, "But I'm a service-based business. I have clients, not products. That won't work for me."

Picture me giving you my best "really" stare.

At this point, I hope all you service-based business owners realize any workshops, ebooks, memberships, or courses you create and offer to your audience are considered products. Yes, I know you work primarily with clients, but if you aren't producing some type of eProduct, we need to talk. You need to have some type of product to help you boost your income. Check out my article "Why every business needs online products," linked in our resource page. I go much deeper into why you should start creating online products. Heck, this book is one of my passive income streams! These income streams are literally the best course of action you can take to create consistent income for your business, without increasing your work hours.

There's also another amazing benefit to creating a budget for service-based businesses. Once you figure out how much you want to make for the entire year, you can figure out how much you'd need to make a month. That then boils down to figuring out how many clients you need to take on each month and at what price. If you want to make $12,000 in a year, then you need to make $1,000 a month. You only want to take on two clients, which means you will need to charge both of them $500 to make your goal. See how simple that is? If you want to up your income, you need to up your prices.

Back to the budget - we've figured out your expenses for each month and total for the year. We've made projections on what we need and want to earn from all of our upcoming projects. We know how many customers need to purchase our products in order to make the income we want. We convinced you to start making passive income products (that was the last one, I swear).

Now, it's time to put it all together, it's time to figure out your financial strategy for the year. I'll wait for you to work on that before I continue. Don't skip ahead and say "Oh, I'll just do it later. I don't even have everything together yet." Go get it together now. Doooo it.

I told you not to skip this.

Shame on you.

Do it.

You'll thank me later.

You're such a rebel.

You totally didn't do it, did you?

I'm begging you. Don't put this off.

Your business will improve drastically once you know your numbers.

Okay, I'm done pleading with you now. Either you did or you didn't. Either way, I have to keep going.

Goals & the Million Ways to Make Them

Chapter Nine

SO FAR, WE'VE EXPERIENCED our passion, gotten our business organized, determined the tools and software we're going to use, and got a budget set up. You've made some hasty goals, which look good on paper. You're ready to go right? Not quite. Let's take a step back and check out those goals. It may not seem like making goals requires a lot of brain power or a big strategy, but it does. If you make your goal to earn $15,000 in the first month of business, you're going to feel discouraged and bad when it doesn't happen. You need to create realistic goals to help move you and your business forward. It keeps you in the right mindset and helps keep things in perspective. While making goals should not be done hastily, it is also something you shouldn't get hung up on.

Imagine if someone had to count the methods you could use to set a goal. They would probably reach somewhere in the millions - oh, and also hate their life, because that job would suck. Which is why I'm not going to go through every option. If you decide to dive into that rabbit hole, there are millions of articles, videos, and tools to go over. Any one of these methods can help you accomplish your goals.

Problems begin to arise when someone starts to believe one of these methods is better than all the rest. They believe they need to find the method which will ensure their success and the accomplishment of their goals. They jump from method to method because they believe they have yet to find the perfect method which will give them a 100% goal completion. Hopefully, you realize there's no such thing. Every person thinks, learns, and works differently. Therefore, each person will be motivated and encouraged to complete their goals in entirely different ways, during entirely different seasons in their life.

It can be tempting to keep trying them all. I mean you spent eight hours setting up the last way, making sure it was pretty and you had all the information exactly the right way. Then you found this method that so-and-so uses and has success with, so of course, this is going to work better for you. Your life is finally going to be exactly what you wanted because you found this new method. These eight hours getting it set up are what is needed to set yourself up for success. It's worth it. When it's all done, you race to post your accomplishment online because it would be selfish of you to not share it with people who might get inspired by it. Then you see someone who has already accomplished several of her goals using a different method you had no idea about. It makes so much more sense than the one you're using now…

Is this starting to sound familiar to anyone?

I want you to take a minute to ask yourself a few questions:

- How long have you been using your current goal setting method?
    - If it's less than a month, why not challenge yourself to use it everyday for a month?
- Do I absolutely despise my current goal setting method?
    - If the answer to this is yes and you've been feeling uninspired, change. Now. Even if it's been less than a month.
    - If the answer is no, not really, try sticking it out for a little bit longer.
- Is there something about my goal setting method that's missing?
    - If yes, what is it? Do you absolutely need it? Are you able to live without it?
- Have I actually used this goal setting method to get closer to my goals?
    - Have you taken action on anything you've set up?
    - Have you made any progress whatsoever toward your goals?

Are you starting to get maybe it's not your goal setting method, but the action you need to take toward accomplishing them - or rather, lack of action you've been taking? It's time to stop blaming the method or tool you use and turn the microscope on yourself. It turns out your lack of success is a result of you and everything you do, say, think, and feel. It's a scary thought when you realize you could go from scrambling for clients and income to having more than you could possibly need. When I realized it, I had a bit of a freak out moment. I was an actual business owner. How weird is that?!

Let's get back to goals. In the blogging universe, a large emphasis is placed on achieving a certain number of page views each month. While it is an important metric to track, unless you are only blogging, you're going to need more than that. To run your business, like the freelancer you are, you need to know how many clients you want to have and how many products you need to sell. Remember when we budgeted and found out you need to have 28 people purchase your $40 product to make the income you need and want?

Well, that's a goal you need to incorporate. Having a goal for how many and what type of products you want to release will help you get passed begging for pageviews and into the role of a business owner. It's how you go from making no money to having an income. Maybe even earning extra money you can use to grow your business.

I have two goal setting methods to share with you. The first one is one of the most prolific goal-creating techniques around. It's hard to believe there are people who have gone their whole lives without seeing this method, but apparently there are. It feels like it's everywhere. This doesn't mean there's anything wrong with it. In fact, I've used it several times. This method helps get you started when you have no idea how to. It keeps it simple and easy to remember. If you've never made any goals before - even if you went goal-making happy and are overwhelmed or frustrated, sit down and go through this method.

It's called the S.M.A.R.T. Technique. Not very cool, huh? Hear me out, if we're really trying to make goals in a way in which we had a decent chance of accomplishing them, this would probably be one of the top techniques recommended. For those who have never heard of this (again, where have you been?), let me break it down.

S - Specific
M - Measurable
A - Achievable
R - Realistic

T - Timely

Basically, in order to make S.M.A.R.T. goals, you need a goal to be specific, able to actually be achieved, in a specific time frame which fits your needs, and with a measurement to know when you've achieved it. Let's work with an example. Say your goal is to write and complete an Ebook for your business. It's a 20 chapter book, complete with a few worksheets. You need to write it and get it up for sale in your online shop, but you're overwhelmed with where to start. Let's take it through the S.M.A.R.T. system.

Specific - finish writing ebook
Measurable - 20 chapters
Achievable - is writing 20 chapters something you can actually do?
Realistic - if you have 4 clients, a ton of deadlines, and a family to take care of, will you be able to write this ebook?
Timely - need it done in 2 months

Put it all together now: Your goal is to write a 20 chapter ebook in 2 months. This breaks down into 10 chapters a month or around 2 - 3 chapters a week. See how the number got smaller and easier to digest? Now let's say you wanted to buffer in a few weeks for editing, so that means you need to do 12 chapters in your first month and you have 8 chapters in your second month, with the time to edit the ebook once or twice. It's supposed to be this easy to set the goal. It's supposed to motivate you to get started. Sitting frozen at a 20 chapter ebook goal isn't going to help you accomplish anything. Breaking down big goals and making them into manageable small steps you can take is the key to goal setting and success.

The next method of goal setting I use is one actually developed by Sarra Cannon. She has a wonderful course, linked in the resource center, everyone should take because it's a ton extremely helpful information. The basis of method is setting a goal, breaking it down into projects, and then breaking it down even further into tasks.

Let's take our 20 chapter ebook. The goal is actually going to be a bit broader: Publish passive income products to increase monthly income by $100/$500/$1,000 by December 31, 2018. This is a goal you don't really have any control over. You do everything in your power to meet the goal, but there's no guarantee. This is an actual goal. You're reaching for it.

The projects for this goal are what you need to

focus on. Each project should have multiple steps under it. If you write down something and it includes a single action, it's not a project - it's a task. So list out all of your projects. It could look something like this: write ebook, edit ebook, format ebook, promote ebook, and release ebook. Each one of these include multiple steps. Writing the ebook project breaks down into tasks like this: write chapter one, write chapter two, or write 1,000 words, write 2,000 words. All of this helps you create task lists you can use to build out your daily and weekly schedule.

Goals don't have to be hard. They don't need to be this Big Scary Thing. They can be small and manageable. Creating these goals is all about developing the right mindset and going forward in a way that your subconscious can get on board with. It's the best way to actually accomplish them. That's the whole point of setting goals, right? To accomplish them. Don't be discouraged. I believe you can do it!

Building a CRM

Chapter Ten

IF YOU DON'T KNOW what CRM stands for, you haven't been paying close attention. CRM stands for Customer Relationship Management. It's an approach to managing a company's interactions with current and potential customers. The way I like to explain it is it's a history record for your company. Every email, piece of paper, and action you do gets recorded. Building a CRM gives you a database of information which will help you not only be the best business owner, but also a great relationship person.

Getting started building a CRM can be daunting. Not only are there a multitude of options of how to build it, but they all have slightly different features at all kinds of prices. Not to mention, you're collecting a ton of information. The best way to navigate everything is to do your research and stay organized. There are plenty of tools and methods to choose from. You need to know what you're looking for. If you want a ton of fancy features, automation, and the like, then a free CRM is probably not going to give you what you need. If you want some of the simple tools to just keep track of everyone's contact information and the last time you spoke with them, then a free tool will be perfect for you.

Having some way to track your clients, your communication, and the progress of it all will help streamline your business and keep you sane. It can also increase your sales if you use it right! A CRM is the lifeline your business needs to truly be successful.

When you first get started with a CRM, you're going to be stuck. There is so much information which needs to be included. Not only do you need to add the individual's name and information, but you need all of the emails, texts, and messages previously exchanged, along with any and all documents. You need to remember all of the conversations you've had previously and any important information they've shared with you so you can add it to their profile. That is a lot of data! Especially when you're doing this for every single person you've met in your business. Just thinking about putting this together probably makes you want to give up on the whole project. These last few sentences have probably convinced you to avoid having a CRM of any kind. Listen, putting in the effort to create this database is worth it. Stick with me and you'll get through this just fine.

Remember, having this database creates a literal history of your business. You know who you've talked with and who was interested in what. You can keep track of everyone who's requested a quote and follow up with them periodically. You are able to outshine your competition when you remember a client's birthday or send a gift out of appreciation. You'll be able to keep track of who you're actually working with and where you are in the projects. You'll be follow-up royalty. You know what they say: the sale is in the follow-up.

There are several ways you can go about getting this setup. You can use a weekend and spend every second getting it set up. Spend this weekend working about 10 hours a day inputting information into a software. It's tedious and mind numbing work. It absolutely sucks while you're doing it. You'll be miserable during it and it will be a hefty project, but when you get it done and have the majority of it ready to use, you'll be so glad you did it. You'll have a whole database at your fingertips, ready to be utilized and grow your business. You won't be stuck halfway between using and not using this tool. You'll be ready to hit the ground running.

Your next option is to get someone else to do it. Hire a Virtual Assistant (VA) and let them go through the misery of setting it up. Give them access to everything and let them deal with it. You will end up with a mostly complete database without the headache of having to stare at a screen for eight hours straight. You should spend some time going through each of the contacts and adding any additional information you need, but the majority of this project will be completed. You'd only be adding in details. This project is either going to cost you money or time. No matter whether you choose to do it yourself or delegate it out, you will lose one of those valuable resources. Figure out which is most valuable to you at this stage in your life and business. Make your decision based off where you're at at this moment.

The third and final option is NOT recommended. The reason I'm adding it is so you have all of the information. Just know, I don't like it. I don't support it. I wish I wasn't adding it, but, I want to be honest and give you all the available options. I still don't like it. The third option is to do it a little at a time. Pick the tool you want to use one week, get the tool set up the next week, import all of your contacts another week, clean up the contacts another week, and then start adding in all of the content as you have time. It's more of an ever-evolving option.

The reason I don't believe anyone should use this option is because you'll never actually work on it as much as it needs. I made the mistake of using this method the first time I tried setting up my CRM. I set up the tool and imported all of my Google contacts, but the information was messed up. I got duplicate contacts for most of them, didn't have any names on others, and got contacts I didn't even need. The information was mostly wrong or missing. It was a mess. I told myself I'd work on it when I got the chance. I never got the chance. There was always something else "more important" to work on.

It took me over six months to actually realize this was a tool I needed to set up and start to utilize. I knew it was important to do, but I just didn't want to have to do it. I had other things that needed my attention first.

Finally, I scheduled a weekend when my fiancé was out of town and made myself sit down and work on it. You may be thinking "Well, I'm different. I won't make the same mistake. I'll get it done." You'd be wrong. There isn't much more I can do to convince you. All I can do is offer a judgement free space to come back to.

When you're ready to get started, come back to this page. I won't condone you bending the corner of the page, but there's a free bookmark PDF in our resources webpage. Print it out and stick it in this chapter for when you want to return. Now that I've saved you from becoming a vicious corner-folding fiend, I want to help you set up your CRM. Most of them allow you to add your own categories or customize them in the way you'd like. It sounds appealing when you're looking for a tool to use, but when it comes time to start creating those categories your mind will go suspiciously blank. I have a feeling it does this on purpose.

Ignoring your suspicious brain for a second, figure out what information you'd like to have on hand. As a service-based business, the information I'm going to need is completely different from the information a product-based business needs. For instance, I do not need their address or size or color-choice. Depending on the product you sell, you might need that information. It helps to take a look at your business model and figure out what information you need and what would be nice to have. Also, if you don't have this information already, send out a survey or questionnaire to all of your clients/customers. Ask them to pretty please fill it out because you're updating your records. You want to make sure they are on your list because they are too important to you not to have them!

Disclaimer: The custom fields I share here are based on when I was using PipeDrive as my main CRM software. If you'd like to see what fields I'm currently using in Streak CRM, check out my set up video in our resources webpage.

Here's my list of custom fields:

Name
Organization
Phone
Email
Birthday
Address
Spouse

Spouse's Birthday

Website

Group

Referred by/How We Met

Notes

Let's do a quick rundown of everything. I keep the client's address to be able to send a birthday card or present. This helps increase brand loyalty. I also include their spouse and their spouse's birthday to do the same. A word of caution: if you have never met your client's spouse and you've never talked about them in any of your conversations, please don't send them a card. That's a bit weird and sends up red flags for your customer.

Next is the group's field. I include this to add the contacts into groups to make it easy to find them. The groups I created are client, partner, guest poster, and event. If I met them at a networking event, I throw them in the event group and write exactly which event in the referred by/how we met section.

In the notes section, I write down any conversations we've had, any emails exchanged, information I've been given - things such as any allergies so I don't send anything they might be allergic to. I add documents, images, and any audio files I may have. This is the bulk of the database. It's where your history with your contacts starts to build and come alive.

Having this information at your fingertips allows you to continue your conversations with your contacts, instead of having to start over in each conversation. This allows the relationship to progress much more quickly than if you went by memory. Do you see the benefit of building this massive information hub? Don't dismiss how impactful information can be. It's the new commodity of the information age. Use it to your advantage.

Websites

Chapter Eleven

THIS CHAPTER WAS ONE I considered taking out altogether. It is a bit controversial in I have an unusual take on websites. I also didn't know how beneficial this chapter would be, as most people form an opinion and don't really change it, but I figured it's a topic we all deal with and having information is always a good thing.

Let's tackle my controversial opinion first. I don't believe you need a website to be a successful entrepreneur. In fact, I know you don't need one. I didn't use a website after month four of my entrepreneurial journey. I'm going to detail out the positives and negatives associated with having a website and not having a website. This way, you can make an informed decision.

We're going to take a look at what it's like when you have a website. The benefit of having a website is you have some place to send people. It's a physical location people can access from anywhere, at any time. It's something people have come to expect a business to have. It can be great to bring in tons of traffic and potential leads. Not to mention, websites can help cut through a lot of the back and forth taking place in emails.

Another benefit to having a website is having a place to share your voice and message. You're able to build a blog or platform you can use to share your knowledge. You can house any digital products or courses you're planning on offering. Having a website definitely has its benefits.

A website can also have drawbacks. Not only are you investing money into this platform, but you're investing time. Even if you're only paying $20 a month, you're putting a good chunk of change into an online window store. Plus, every time you update it, revamp it, or do anything to improve it, you're investing your time. This is time which can be used to pitch new clients, nurture a relationship with a potential client, or work on any client projects you may have.

Having this website doesn't mean you'll gain more clients. In fact, I found my website mostly sat there with no traffic coming in. I received exactly zero clients from my website and yet, I was paying $20 a month for nothing. Spending three months building a website you'll pay for every month and won't bring in any additional clients is one of the most common practices new freelancers partake in. It's also a big negative of having a website. Remember, no traffic means you won't have an audience to buy any of your digital products or courses.

Maybe you're seriously considering having a website or maybe you're contemplating what it would be like without one. Why would it be a good idea <u>not</u> to have a website? Not only would you be foregoing the monthly expense of a digital placeholder, but you'd also avoid a productive procrastination method. You wouldn't be able to procrastinate by working on making your website perfect and feeling productive. You'd be forced to focus on building your client roster.

Not only will not having a website free up your time and funds, it will force you to be clearer and more involved in the selling process with potential clients. Now, you won't be dismissing them and sending them to an impersonal, un-interactive website, which answers none of their questions and only frustrates them. Now, you'll be there for them every step of the way. They will have a live person to work with, build a relationship with, and turn to anytime they want to purchase more services.

Not having a website can be difficult. Like I mentioned before, many people have come to expect one. It throws people off when you say you don't have one. You'll end up with a lot more emails in your inbox because you're having to answer so many questions a website can answer. Plus, there's the problem of not having a naturally built-in platform to house your digital products and courses.

It can get a bit awkward when someone asks for your website and you say you don't have one. A moment of panic can easily rise up when this happens. I know it did the first time I went through it. To combat the awkwardness and panic, it helps to have your whole answer prepared. For instance, when someone asks me for my website, I say, "I actually don't have a website since I hand pick all of my clients so I can deliver the best possible value. I do have samples I'd love to send you." This gives potential clients a natural segway to move the conversation forward and shows I'm trying to provide the best value.

If you decide to make a website, there are a few things you should keep in mind. The first thing is building a website doesn't have to be this big huge thing you're terrified of. Take it one step at a time. Use all the resources you have to help you get through each step. Things like other websites, books, and tutorial videos can make creating a website a snap. It doesn't matter what your website looks like. It matters it's complete, it has the information your potential clients might need, and it looks like you've put some effort and time into it. The main thing you have to remember when it comes to online businesses is the design and content are not permanent. You can always change your website if you end up hating it.

While every website is different and what you feel is important will be different, there are several things every website should include. Again you will add them onto your website very differently than I did, but you should really have it somewhere there. These are things the public has come to expect to find on a website, no matter whose it is or what it's for. If you don't have this information, written in plain English and easy to read, then you're going to lose your readers - and fast.

Here's what should be on your website:

A contact page - I see so many business owners have beautiful websites with amazing images, beautifully written copy, and products I'm ready to buy, but have no contact information. If you want clients, you have to let them know how they can work with you!

A tag line - this can be in the form of your mission statement, a tag line, or a sentence. It needs to state who you are in business for and what you do to help them. This is how you make sure the right clients are reaching out.

Start here page - this is a page to direct new readers to. This helps give your readers a place to learn a bit about how your business works and what to expect. It also helps cut through overwhelm when landing on a new website with a ton of information. It gives them a place to start.

About You/Business - This can be about either you or your business story, but it needs to really show a potential client what to expect. There shouldn't be stiff, completely formal copy when you conduct business in a more relaxed, informal manner.

Services/Shop - putting all of this time and effort into making a website for potential clients means you're looking to gain clients. Duh. Don't you think they should know what you're offering to them? They won't buy anything unless you tell them what you're offering. What's even better is offering them the option to actually buy it on the website.

These are optional, but good ideas to add to your website:

In the news - places people can find you or your products/services mentioned in the news or written about.

Portfolio - this is a good page to have when you direct potential clients, but your website shouldn't be only a portfolio. It is a live interactive site which needs to be regularly updated with content.

Your Prices - this is a rather controversial topic, but I believe you shouldn't add prices onto your site. I know it may seem odd, but adding prices onto your website locks you into a box. Even if you say the prices "start at" a certain number, people will hard ball you into offering that price for everything you do.

Blog - adding in a blog onto your website gives you better SEO results (more about that below), adds to your authority, and gives your audience a reason to regularly visit your website. It also gives you more time being the center of their attention and thus can lead to more sales.

There are plenty of other aspects which can be added onto a website. Things like a sidebar, a search bar, or a page of frequently asked questions are always helpful. It all depends on what you think is important for your readers to experience. Take your time in figuring out what you believe needs to be added. If your business model is a bit difficult or you have a completely new process for onboarding clients, explain it. If you're offering any freebies, you need to create landing pages for them (again, we're talking about this in a later chapter). If you're focused on video, you may want to add in a video section. Creating your website shouldn't take six months, but you certainly shouldn't force yourself to make a "perfect" one in a matter of days or weeks either.

Your website should be a living breathing thing. It's not meant for you to set up and then walk away. Update it, post blogs to it, and change up your pictures. The more updates your website gets, the better SEO it will have. Posting a weekly blog post helps keep your SEO optimized. If you're going to put all of this time into creating and paying for your website, you should keep it as updated and easily searchable as possible.

For those who have no idea what SEO is or how it works, I'm including a mini lesson.

What is SEO?
SEO stands for search engine optimization. It basically means you're making your website easy to find through search engines, a.k.a. Google.

What does it mean to have Google "ping" my site?
It means Google is searching your site to find keywords that people are looking for. It means Google is combing through each one of your pages and finding information

and content it thinks the public will like and enjoy when they search for something relevant.

How does Google ping my site?
Search engines like Google basically crawl your website looking for specific things in order to establish your authority and authenticity.

What does Google look for?
Things like complex keywords, labeled image files, headers with straight forward descriptions, and descriptions on your pages, site, and images. Each page has 1 - 2 sentences explaining what it's about with a few complex keywords in the header description.

And complex keywords are?
2 - 5 keywords which explain who you are and what you do. Instead of photographer or even newborn photographer, you're the San Diego-based newborn photographer. You add this into your site a few times and Google picks up on it.

You've learned what to put on your website, what SEO is

and how to use it. Now, it's time to get it set up. You'll need a domain before you do anything. You'll need to make sure your domain isn't taken already. This is where you need to get creative, but make sure you have a domain which is easy to remember. It also needs to be easy to type into an iPhone. Nobody has time to type out 32 letters into that tiny screen.

Next, I'd suggest setting up your business email. While it may not seem vital to getting a website set up, it actually is the backbone of your business. You'll need someplace to send all of your client and online account emails. We already talked about this in Chapter 5, but this is such an important step it warranted repeating. Get an email and one you would be comfortable sharing with the CEO of Apple. You definitely don't want to send an email to him from gigglepantscuddleparty72@yahoo.com so make sure you get a business account and are comfortable with it. You'll be stuck with this email forever. There really isn't any other way to change it, other than starting a whole new email address, but really, who wants to deal with that hassle?

Once you have your domain and your email, you need to figure out where you want to build your website. There are plenty of options and plenty more articles written about each of them. This isn't a decision you should take lightly. You'll be building the face of your business on this website. I know we discussed not using a website at all, but since you insisted on doing this, you should probably put some effort into it. You don't want to have to rebuild your entire site after you finished designing the whole thing. You should be focusing on getting clients. This means you should research all of the different platforms and determine which one works best for you and your situation <u>before</u> you do all this work.

    Building a website is going to take you some time. The hard part of it all is you literally have a blank canvas to work with. You need to make a decision about every box placement and image showcase. The fun part is you literally have a blank canvas to work with. You get to make every decision. The first one starts with where to build it. The platform you use can determine what your frustration level will be stationed at throughout the duration of the project. For someone like me, WordPress kept my frustration level in the "I'm going to throw this laptop and then set it on fire" zone. Which isn't a great place to be. This is when knowing what each platform's pros and cons are can help you choose the best path for you.

    SquareSpace and WordPress are two of the larger

website hosts. While there are literally dozens more, those two are the popular ones. Obviously I have a favorite - you already know what my relationship with WordPress looked like. This doesn't mean I think it's better or even the right platform for everyone. It was the platform which worked best for me. It cut my frustration level from the "I'm going to throw this laptop and then set it on fire" zone down to the "I'm so confused and frustrated, but I'm going to take a break and get back to it later" zone. This is a tremendously big difference in how I dealt with the two platforms! If you can learn things easily and understand coding, WordPress may not be a bad option. Like I said, depending on who you are and what you provide, there may be a clear-cut path for you.

SquareSpace is a simple drag-and-drop software. Like I said, you don't have to know any type of coding for this platform. You have the option to add coding and customize the website to your preferences, but it is not necessary at all. They've got some great customer service and are adding new templates and features every day. The negative about SquareSpace is you start with a template. While this works for someone like me with no experience in coding, people who know how to code hate SquareSpace because you can't make it your own. You can add simple code into it, but if you add too much, it may mess up your mobile view or break the sync all together.

Another thing is while you still own the rights to your content, SquareSpace has the power to shut your website down and essentially hold your content hostage. That being said, don't do stupid things that will cause your website to be shut down. You're building a business, not out to "make a name for yourself" like some sort of wannabe rapper looking to make it big.

On the other end of the spectrum, WordPress is a great website host. We established you will need some coding skills, time to dedicate to setting it up, and an understanding about how plugins work. If you have all of that, you will have access to everything you've ever wanted in your dream website. It can literally look like and do anything you need it to do, if you know how to use it to its fullest extent.

The ability to customize and add virtually anything you desire makes this platform highly appealing. It's awesome because if you want to add a store or change the way your site looks, you can change everything. You can make it look exactly the way you want it to. It can seem overwhelming to make every single choice about whether there should be content or blank space, but when the product is done, you will be so proud. That being said, you need to make sure you add a deadline to building and messing with this. I don't want your entire first year in business to have all been focused on building a website, with no leads or clients anywhere.

Building a website is a big process. It shouldn't be something you take on lightly, but it shouldn't be something you spend forever on. You need to focus on building a business, not a website. This means you need to focus on finding and signing clients. Not on making sure your website has the perfectly sized header. You need to build a client base, create products to offer, and so on. Make your decisions quickly and focus on creating a website which has pertinent information, gives someone a reason to come back, and showcases the message you're wanting to share. It's not a reason for you to bury your head in the website making trenches.

Have I convinced you to stop making a "perfect" website yet?

Style Your Copy to Improve Your Brand

Chapter Twelve

COPY IS SUCH A vague and important sounding term. It scares off a ton of people with its importance. It basically means every single place your audience will read words you've published, from social media texts to full books. It is crucial to style your copy so it correctly shares your message. This means your copy needs to reflect your brand's style. It isn't difficult to style your words, but it's important to stay consistent. You want to make sure you know who you're talking with and what they hear you saying.

The first decision you need to make in styling your copy is what kind of style will you be speaking in? For businesses like lawyers, those in the health sector, and anyone in academia circles, you may want to opt for more formal styles. This means using buzz words, providing ample evidence for any claims you bring forth and avoiding contractions.

It means keeping your opinion pretty much out of the whole document and focusing on the facts and relevant information on the topic you're speaking about. For bloggers, creative types, and coaches, styles are more casual. This means using shorter, simpler words, keeping the sentences short and casual, and bringing in obscure, yet hilarious references to showcase your point.

The main difference between formal writing styles and more casual styles is mainly the use of contractions. For instance, the sentence "I will provide all the details and resources you need for this conference next week" is pretty formal. It's something you'll expect to hear in an office building or near someone with four Ph.D.'s. It becomes more casual when you add a contraction - "I'll provide all the details and resources you need for this conference next week." This is copywriter's big secret.

Using contractions swings the writing style from formal to casual and back faster than any word choices. Of course, the sentence can become even more casual: "I'll give you everything for the conference next week." It's all a matter of conveying your thoughts in the style you want your business to be best known for.

Styling your copy is a great way to brand your business. It's one more tool you can use to expand and solidify your brand. For instance, you may want to appear "cool" and be the business known for being blunt. In that case, you may add in some cuss words. If you are playing more with the themes, you can add metaphors and puns which speak to those themes. If you want to be known as relatable, you can add in references to experiences a large part of the population has been through - high school, parents being upset, embarrassment, or having a great book to read.

If you really want to sound like an experienced writer, there are three simple tricks you can implement in two minutes. I love sharing these because ever since I started incorporating them into my writing, I've found others are astounded at how "amazing" I write and it's all because of these simple hacks. The first hack is to stop using the word "that" in your writing. Instead of "I explained to her that she needed a ticket," write it as "I explained to her she needed a ticket." See how the second sentence can communicate the message much clearer?

My next hack is taking the word "just" out of your writing. Not to make this a gender thing, but it's a big habit women need to get rid of. Instead of sending an email saying "just checking in," you should write something like "wanted to check in" or literally "checking in." You don't have to add in the word "just." In fact, when you're writing to males, they find this an insecure move and in fact, it is! Every time you use the word just, you're diminishing the work you do, the power you have, and the confidence you have in yourself. Stop it!

My third hack is deleting two more words from your writing - the words "I think" need to go. Stop thinking! Start doing! You don't think something should happen - you know. Look at this sentence, "I think it's time to create a new workflow." It's a much stronger sentence when you say "It's time to create a new workflow." There's no question in the second sentence. It's time, no thinking or wondering or pondering. It's time, that's it. Using the words "I think" is another form of insecurity and is another method used to diminish your value. Again, stop it!

These are simple fixes, but deleting these phrases and words from your vocabulary instantly raises your authority, value, and confidence. This isn't something you should consider doing. Do it. You want to be a badass boss? You want to be a kickass expert? Take these words out of your vocabulary. From this point on, these words will not enter your writing.

Use the worksheet in our resource center to create a guide for your style. This will keep your style consistent and in line with the branding you're wanting to portray. Every time you start to write something, whether it be a sales page, a blog post, or even a social media post, use your worksheet to guide your writing. This keeps you from writing in different styles, plus it has the added benefit of eliminating any writer's block you may have. This isn't a worksheet you fill out and then file away. Keep it at the forefront of your business! Keep a copy on your desktop. Tape a copy up in your office. Do whatever you need to, but keep this document up to date and easily accessible.

When you are speaking in one voice, your audience has an easier time telling who you are. They trust you more, find you relatable, and actually want to buy from you. It doesn't matter what type of style you use in your business - it needs to be one and the same, throughout every part of your business. It's all about staying true to your message and your brand. You don't want your audience to be confused as to who is talking to them. When you speak (write, post, etc.), you want them to know who you are.

Marketing Your Services

Chapter Thirteen

THE WORLD HAS EVOLVED. We've evolved from an industrial world to an informational world. You already know this because we talked about it earlier, but I firmly believe this can't be said enough. In this communication revolution, marketing is vital. Marketing is how you share what your business does to people who are looking for what you offer, in the way you offer it. Marketing tells the world exactly why they need what you have, what and how you offer it, and where they can get it. To be successful at marketing, all you need to do is share a cohesive consistent message. You don't want to confuse your audience by sharing a message which goes against everything you value or says it in a way they don't understand.

Marketing your services is important. It's not hard to understand the concept or why it's necessary. What's hard to get a grasp on is how to actually do it and do it well. It takes a lot of work to get everything set up and can make the process overwhelming. It got to the point where I stopped wanting to try. I was confused because everywhere I turned, I was being told something different. Make email marketing your priority. Focus on building your social media profiles. Don't even worry about social media, you should be building up a blog. Keep your focus on video. It changed every time I turned around and probably changed twice while I was facing the other way, considering the speed new technology is coming out. Then, I discovered some amazing resources which made everything clear and easy to understand.

One of these amazing resources is Lisa Jacobs of Marketing Creativity. She not only makes the selling, but the buying process fun and easy to learn about. I use her Your Best Year Productivity workbook in order to organize my business and get my marketing and my product production together. Because of her, her workbooks, and all the other products I've bought from her (there's been a lot), my business has flourished. I was able to learn exactly what the buying process is and how it works. I was able to learn how to launch my first course and got practice building a full marketing campaign. I spend a ton of time reading her emails, watching her videos, and buying her products. You should too.

You already know the best resource I've ever found - in the world: Jenny and Alex. These two are, by far, the be-all, end-all resources you'll need. If you want to build any type of business, be it a service business or a product business, you need to listen to these two women. It not only made my business come alive, but following their teachings actually gave me a business!

Before them, I made exactly $17 after two years of never-ending work. Because of Jenny and Alex, I made over $3,000 in my first year! I know this number isn't super impressive, but to someone who literally did no business before finding them, that was a big jump. I am now on my way to having regular $5,000 months! Soon, it will be $10,000 months and it's only going up from there.

If I could only give you one piece of advice in this entire book, it would be to learn everything you can from Jenny and Alex.

Okay, I'll stop singing their praises long enough to finish this chapter. I can't promise they won't come up again. #girlcrushtothemax

Moving on, here's a few marketing terms you'll need to learn and love. They are prevalent in every aspect of business - in every industry. They are words which have changed a lot of the typical business scene. Their meanings change seemingly everyday. They are scary, broad, and incredibly annoying because they are everywhere. Learn to embrace them and what they can do for your business.

You have no choice:

Email Marketing
Landing Page
Social Media Marketing
Sales Funnel
Call to Action

Blogging

E-Commerce

Inbound Marketing

This isn't even close to all of the terms you'll need to learn. This is, however, a list of some of the most frustrating terms most entrepreneurs have trouble defining and implementing into their business. Every time you hears these terms, you're going to want hock a 50 pound bag of flour at the person who thought up these *special* terms. I promise, once you get the basics down, you'll end up ignoring these high-touting terms and focus on the basic definitions, which is the only thing you really need to know.

There are several hundred million articles, books, and videos addressing what each of these topics are and how they can impact a business. Seriously, there have been some intense debates about the meanings and how they should be applied in different industries. It's awesome to see these words can mean completely different things and nobody can actually agree on them. I'm going to include a small definition so you aren't completely confused and we have some sort of basis to work with. These terms are necessary for you to know going forward, but I'd take some time to dive in further, if I was you.

Email Marketing - this is the general term used for marketing and advertising products or services to everyone who subscribed to receive email updates from you. It involves sales funnels, landing pages, marketing campaigns, and so much more. The basis of it is you send out emails in a sequence which provides value and education to your subscribers with a few opportunities to purchase your products, services, etc.

Landing Pages - this is where all of the information about your program, services, and so on goes. It is a page your potential customers land on to learn in-depth, detailed information about a certain offering you have available. These pages lead to the payment screen where someone can purchase your offering or book a phone call to learn more. It's the "landing" point which gives potential customers/clients reasons why they should purchase and offers them the opportunity to buy.

Social Media Marketing - as much as you don't want to have to deal with social media, you lost that argument quite a few years ago. If you aren't using social media to your advantage, you're missing out immensely. There are too many opportunities being offered through social channels for you not to be involved. Social media marketing is essentially using social media platforms of your choosing to market your brand and give value, information, and opportunities to buy from you.

Sales Funnel - this is a fun little word everyone seems to throw around for all sorts of reasons. Nobody really seems to break this down. In a nutshell, a sales funnel is the process a potential customer takes from finding your landing page to signing up for your email list to actually purchasing from you. Most funnels consistent of anywhere from 8 - 15 emails to really provide value to customers before asking for a sale. In essence, it's the funnel you take new audience members through to take them from "new follower" to "loyal customer."

Call to Action - You may have seen this referred to as your CTA, but for your emails, posts, and any other content you publish, you want to make sure you're including a call to action. Basically this means you've asked a question, asked them to do something, or included some type of call to get your audience to take some kind of action. Most of the time, your CTA should be a question or "homework" action. Sometimes it will be a call to purchase something from you. Other times, it will be to get them to think about a specific topic or check something out. The majority of what you publish should have some type of CTA, although DO NOT shove it down your audience's throats. If it doesn't feel authentic or right, don't include in every post. Scatter it around and try it in different versions/styles.

Blogging - I'm sure you know what blogging means, but I included it because there are many types and ways to blog. While most blogs are housed on traditional websites, many use secondary sites to spread their message. Blogging on Instagram, LinkedIn, or sites like Medium are all new forms of blogging which have grown in popularity. Don't dismiss these platforms because they aren't traditional. If you spend more of your time on LinkedIn, then use it to your advantage. Make sure you have a content strategy, write your posts early, and include bright, beautiful imagery (THAT YOU HAVE PERMISSION TO USE) and you'll see some ROI in no time.

Branding - While this term doesn't have any marketing actions associated with it, it is vital to marketing success. When marketing online, branded images, logos, and copy is incredibly important. There are millions of people online. You want to make sure it's easy to spot your brand among them. The brand you create shows customers what to expect from you and who you really are. It is the promise of an experience and you need everything you publish to help sell that promise.

E-Commerce - This topic is incredibly broad. Boiling it down, it can be summed up in a few words. E-Commerce is the act of selling items or services online. It is the idea of having an online "store." At the core, it literally means electronic commerce or money on the Internet. Yes, it seems intimidating, but creating an E-Commerce site just means you're offering products/services to purchase online.

Inbound Marketing - This term sounds intimidating too! I promise, it sounds much scarier than it actually is. Inbound marketing refers to the points of your business where you are bringing in a new audience member. Those points can include publishing content and updating platforms regularly. Things like a blog, YouTube channel, and website are all points of inbound marketing. When you create ads on Facebook or share Instagram Stories, you're creating touch points for your audience to come "in" to your business and your brand. It's an introduction point.

Marketing is fun when you know what you're doing and how to do it. I spent most of my first few years "learning" marketing and realizing I had no idea what I was doing. After taking some time to actually learn *how* to market from Lisa, Jenny, and Alex (what, I told you they were going to come up again), it's come to be my favorite part of being in business! It's too much fun to create these introduction points and build a community to not build a sales funnel! While the majority of marketing is going to come directly from your efforts, there are several different avenues you can get involved in to have others help market you and your business.

Aside from buying advertisements in newspapers, magazines, on websites, and such, you're able to market yourself to different audiences when you use different avenues. You may have gotten jobs from people you know or on those pesky content mills you're phasing out, but without marketing yourself through different avenues, all of those jobs will be one-offs. You won't be able to gain any new clients. You'll be stuck before you've even begun.

My favorite way to get new clients is through

pitching, but we'll come back to that.

My favorite way to gain new clients, through marketing efforts specifically, is writing guest posts. I'm a writer so that shouldn't come as a shock. What does come as a shock to other people is how easily I receive opportunities to write guest posts. They always seem to have a hard time finding opportunities to guest post, which baffles me. I've guest posted quite a few times and each time, I used the same method: I asked. I ask who would like me to write a post about "insert topics I'm an expert at teaching." I post this question in Facebook groups, on my social media platforms, and in my newsletter. I end up getting about 10 - 15 requests for posts. I write them, send them off with my headshot and biography, and then promote them on my social media channels once they're published. Not only am I published on someone else's platform, but now they are regularly promoting my post and business on their platforms. It's literally as simple and easy as that.

My second favorite method of advertising my business is interviews! Being interviewed on podcasts, webinars, video episodes, and in virtual summits are all fantastic opportunities for you to gain exposure and showcase your expertise. I gained opportunities to take part in all of these avenues using the same method I used to get guest posts - I asked! My ability to market my business and grow is fueled solely by what I ask for and how often I ask. Therefore, I make sure asking is something I do often!

While all of these avenues are fantastic at getting your business exposure, there is no best method to use. I know it's an answer everyone hates, but it's true. Marketing is not doing one thing over and over - it's the sum of all of your marketing efforts. It's taking all the time and effort you've put into posting on social media, writing guest posts, doing interviews, and creating email campaigns and adding it all together. It's the result of consistently adding value to your community's lives and being someone they can trust.

The best marketing is the marketing which benefits your business the most. It may be one area - it may be all of them. It may be one thing this month and a whole other the next. The point is your business isn't static - your marketing shouldn't be either. Try new things, get creative, and market your business extensively.

Remember - marketing should be something you use consistently, often, and as best as you can, but your focus should be on pitching directly to businesses you want as your clients. You need clients to sustain your business. I like to think of it as two areas of my business: pitching is to get one-on-one clients and marketing is to get customers who will purchase any digital products/courses I produce. This way I have multiple revenue streams and my business is more secure if I decide to slow down pitching or a launch doesn't go so well.

Content Strategy

Chapter Fourteen

THIS IS PROBABLY ONE of my favorite chapters in this whole book. Content strategy is my jam. Marketing as a whole is fun, but there are so many moving parts it can be difficult to keep up with everything. A content strategy dives deep and focuses specifically on how you're going to create content and where you'll be sharing it. It's about making sure you're not only getting the best bang for your buck (time), but you're also spreading the value you offer to your audience in the right way.

The concept of a content strategy isn't hard to understand. It's a fancy word for a very simple process. The confusion comes when you add in all sorts of fancy tools and concepts. You want to simplify the process.

Having this strategy is supposed to help you, not make your life harder. Your content strategy is a guide to stretch the influence your content provides. You are using this strategy to guide you in creating the type of content your audience loves. It isn't meant to keep you in a rigid box. It's meant to help you be flexible and roll with the punches, not freak out because one piece of content isn't exactly the right one.

So, let's start creating your content strategy. Use the worksheet PDF located on our resources page to follow along with us while we create this strategy. If you're not in the position to print/work through this right now, make sure to bookmark this page (no folding corners!) and go through it when you can. This is another worksheet which needs to be a working, fluid document which changes and updates as your business grows. Your content strategy is an action plan for keeping track of all of the content you create and what you want to do with it.

It doesn't help when you've filed that plan away and aren't able to reference it while you're creating content.

The first step is to determine your audience. There are literally hundreds of articles which dictate what you should know about your ideal audience and how deep you should go. I've seen some audience profiles where they get scarily specific. While the idea of getting to know your audience intimately works for some - mostly those who need a crystal clear picture in order to move forward - I operate using a general picture which allows me to imagine all sorts of possibilities.

I write for all types of people. I don't just write to the woman who has graduated college and is looking to create her own business. I write to all the women who are looking to be in this situation or who are going down a different path and are lost. I want my content to be specifically general. I realize this is the most frustrating statement I could have given you and it goes completely against all other advice given, but it works for me. I speak about specific topics. The content I create is focused on getting individuals to a specific outcome, regardless of where they're coming from. The people who read or view my content are there to get action items, tips, tricks, and more. They aren't there so I can speak to one person.

Disclaimer: I am in no way dismissing the concept of audience profiles. My community has been compiled of a large variety of people. I fabricated it this way. For many just starting, focusing on a specific type of individual is much easier than trying to attract several different individuals. Go with what works for you.

The next step is figuring out what topics you'll be writing/creating content about. I know everyone and their mother advocates for picking one niche and focusing on topics which fit. I'm not everybody. I advocate a bit differently, which is totally influenced by Alex and Jenny. I'm not afraid to admit they have been a "bad" influence on me. They are seriously my favorite people ever.

  Instead of niching down to one specific niche and writing about this one topic, choose three to five industries you are truly passionate about. This way you aren't fighting all of the people in one industry. Plus, if and when one of your industries starts a recession, you can shift your focus towards one of your other industries and not have to take a hit in pay! However, I do recommend choosing niches which are somewhat related. You can't pick transportation, stationery/paper supplies, and wildlife. These industries don't relate to each other and publishing content focused on all of these will just confuse your audience. If you're passionate about stationary/paper supplies, then look for surrounding industries, like education or the planner industry. You want to find coordinating niches which support and complement each other. They also need to make sense around each other when you're creating different content.

The justification to niche down includes the argument clients want someone who is specialized in exactly what they are looking for and only that topic. While this argument makes sense, the truth of the matter is your clients don't care what you specialized in. They only care if you can do what they need and do it well. Your abilities are what the clients want, not your specialization. That being said, your skills and samples need to reflect that ability. You can't say you're a technology writer and have nothing to back it up. Create samples you can send to potential clients or find a small project you can do quickly. When they ask for samples, send them only the samples they would be interested in - samples in their industry.

After you finished picking your niches, it's time to identify what type of content each industry audience consumes. For example, if my niches were the planning community, stationery, and office supplies, I'd probably make a ton of video content. All of these industries love to see products, reviews, and ideas on how to utilize different types of products. If I was a technology writer, I'd probably create LinkedIn articles to showcase and market my skills. This industry loves longer articles of 1,000 - 2,000 words. On average, successful companies employ about 15 different content approaches.

Since I've been a solopreneur most of my career, I chose three strategies. I can handle three myself. When I get to the point where I have less time and I have more funds to help me expand, I'll bring someone on and start experimenting with adding other strategies. Marketing needs anything but a one and done approach. It takes creativity, trial, and error.

The main reason you're creating this content strategy is to create a consistent style and voice, and be able to refer back to it. Remember, we created that whole copy style guide? That wasn't just for fun; all of these exercises and templates are tools for you to become the freelancer you've always wanted to be. Most industries, regardless of which one, want the style and voice to reflect highly positive, upbeat content. There is a message of hope and of vulnerability. I share fun content to break up the day which also provides them with some action steps to improve their business. Write out the message you want to share with your audience. This shouldn't be something you agonize over - it's a simple, fluid guideline which represents your brand. Do what feels right for you.

Once you know what type of content you want and what message you're going to be sharing, it's time to creating a posting schedule and calendar. You'll need to determine how often you want to be publishing content. For things like social media updates and blog posts, you should be publishing more frequently. For things like webinars or eBooks, the publishing can be spread out over a month or quarter. Again, this decision is a personal one. If you're a mom of three very active boys, a wife, a pet owner, and a student, you may want to scale back the amount of content you publish. There's absolutely nothing wrong with doing so - it's all based on you and your circumstance. The best suggested publishing guidelines mean nothing if you end up hating your business and feeling guilty because you can't keep up.

Determining how often you want to post allows you to get a calendar started. Say you know you want to publish a blog post once a week. You'll need to schedule four-to-five posts throughout the month. Assigning the dates you want to publish on allows you to determine when you will need them ready by - I'd suggest at least two days before you plan to publish it. This gives you time to edit, format, and find images for the post. Also, knowing when you'll be publishing allows you to determine which order you'd like to share them in.

When you have brainstormed enough ideas, start filling in title details on the dates you want to publish. You'll know which post you need to work on first in order to get it ready for its publication date. This calendar allows you to see the whole year at a glance and gives you the opportunity plan out launch content. This is why I used CoSchedule. It allowed me to easily keep track of all of the posts I was working on, the social media posts I wrote for them, and any launches I was planning.

Take a weekend, spend one full day, take a few months, do whatever works best for you to confidently get this system set up. Use the PDF we mentioned earlier to build your content strategy and create content you're excited about. It is your checklist to keep track of your progress and create a full year's worth of content in a cohesive manner. Each time you decide to launch something, every time a new quarter starts, or you lose track of the message you're trying to share, refer back to this document. This document is your grounding point.

HOW NOT TO BE JUST ANOTHER FREELANCER

Any time you forget why you're doing this, anytime you forget what you're trying to say, reference this document.

Blogs

Chapter Fifteen

WHILE CREATING YOUR CONTENT strategy, you chose which content approaches to utilize. This could be blogging, video content, courses, webinars, email marketing, and so much more! It gets exhausting keeping up with all of them. However, if you didn't include blogging, you should really rethink your strategy.

According to a study compiled by HubSpot in 2015, business-to-business companies that blogged 11+ times per month had almost three times more traffic than those blogging 0-1 times per month. I don't know about you, but three times more traffic means three times more potential clients.

A blog is where I showcase my abilities, share my skills, and give value to my followers. It's where I entice readers to support me and my message. I'm able to share how I've helped my clients and why I'm the best one for the job. My personality is shown through my voice and followers get a feel for how we would work together. It's literally one of the easiest ways to bring in potential clients and screen out the ones who don't enjoy my writing or the way I work.

Now, I've hopefully given you adequate examples thus far in this book of how technologically inclined I am - hint: I'm not. Therefore, I'm not going to attempt to tell you the technical version of setting up your blog. It would be a bunch of mumbo jumbo anyway and we're not here to learn nonsense from me. What we're going to go over is figuring out what should go on it and how to get it started. Should you need technical help, I'd suggest talking to my friend Google.

On to the part I actually know. There aren't many

elements to a blog. Your blog shouldn't be your website homepage. You want your blog to be on your website, but it shouldn't *be* your website. As a personal preference, I'd suggest adding a search bar. It's one of my biggest pet peeves as a reader. I want to be able to search among the potentially thousands of articles you've written and published for a specific subject I want to read. I don't want to have to click the arrows at the bottom of each page and go through 50 pages. That's a waste of my time and if I don't see what I'm looking for by the third or fourth page, I'll end up finding someone else's site. It's helpful to your audience to have some way to search through all of your content for a specific topic or blog post. Be nice to them and let them have that option.

If your website host/theme allows it, adding categories or topics is also a great idea. It gives your audience an idea of what type of articles to expect from you, gives them ideas on what type of topics they can read, and offers more data to gather regarding about content topics they enjoy (and you should create more of). Not to mention, offering categories and topics keeps newcomers from feeling overwhelmed or confused by the amount of content you publish. If you aren't allowed to display the categories or topics you write about, most website providers offer the option to tag all of your posts. Create three to four tags for your website and let those serve as your "categories."

Once you figure out how you want your blog set up and organized, it's time to start brainstorming content. Using the categories you picked out, you can brainstorm topics for each one you went with and create content evenly for each category. If you're writing to the education industry, you'll probably want to make sure you include topics on preparing to educate others, new trends for teaching others, and ideas on how to implement new techniques. It gives the people who are reading your blog the idea they need to come to you for education information because you're the one leading the discussion. There are plenty of places to find topic ideas such as these. If you need help getting ideas, check out my freebie I have housed on our resources page called "25 Places to Find Content Ideas."

Once you have your topics decided upon, start to plan out your editorial calendar. Assign each topic to a specific day - keep going until you've gotten the whole year assigned. Should you have launches or products coming out, include them and articles you've written announcing them, marketing them, and shouting praise for them in your calendar. This isn't a solid calendar. It sucks to hear, but the reality is this is yet another document which will change and update as your business changes. It needs to be fluid. I've kept my editorial calendar in Trello, Google Calendar, and CoSchedule. I've also used a physical planner by putting topics on sticky notes in order to change it up easily.

Once you know which topics you'll be posting and on which dates, you need to brainstorm article ideas. These are the actual articles you'll be writing, like "The Effects of Using Tablets in the Classroom" or "Are You Using This Technique: If Not, You Will Be," not actual articles. I would end up putting these in the dates I wanted to publish them on, so I knew which article was coming up first. Then, I'd write, edit, and format the article, as we mentioned above. This is creating the actual editorial part of your calendar. When you complete this step, you'll have titles in each of the dates you're planning to publish.

I use Google Drive to write out my blog posts. I am definitely a paper and pen type of person, but writing them out on the computer allows me to catch any spelling or grammar mistakes and saves me time. The images used in these blog posts are photos I've taken myself, for the most part. The copyright issue is becoming much more of a big deal, plus I don't want to be the one who has to pay thousands of dollars because I wanted to use a photo I found online. I tend to outline all of my posts, write them all, add photos, schedule them all out, and let them be. This is batching my work and it allows me to work at a much quicker speed because I don't have to focus on doing different tasks every few minutes. I even take the time to write six to seven social media posts for each blog post I create. The posts are added into CoSchedule to be automatically published. This whole process takes me about three to four months to compile and schedule for the entire year.

Blog posts typically range from 300 - 2,000 words. It all depends on your audience. If you don't want to figure out how to write 2,000 words about the new color you introduced for your product, then don't. That's probably best saved for a 300-500 word post anyways. Your audience doesn't care that much about the new color. They want to see a short announcement which tells them what is new, when they're able to purchase it, which items come in the new color, and what else they may expect later. Longer posts tend to be focused on technical information, explaining a new concept, or going into detail about something specific. These posts need the 2,000 words because there is so much information going into them. They break up the posts by adding in several photos throughout the whole article.

Should you be launching a workshop, course, or membership, go back to all of your previously published posts and add a blurb with a sign up button or link to the new page at the end of all of them. This allows you to promote your launch whenever someone reads your article, regardless of whether they're there for your course or not. It kills two birds with one stone and minimal effort. Not to mention it continuously promotes your audience to read more content while learning more about your services/offerings.

Blogging is so important for your business. It brings in regular traffic and eyes to your website - and your offerings. It gives you free advertising, boosts your authority, and is fun! This shouldn't be something you make into a task you hate completing. It should be something you have a little fun with while doing. Include cliches, puns, or bad jokes if that's your thing. Throw in Harry Potter references or share an inside joke only a Whovian would known. This allows you to truly connect with fellow audience members, plus it shows your personality. You're attracting potential customers who enjoy that type of thing and repelling customers who don't mesh with your personality. If you find you end up hating blogging, stop. Again, this is to fit your business

HOW NOT TO BE JUST ANOTHER FREELANCER

and make it so you can market your business, your way.

KAYLEE WHITE

Newsletters and Social Media

Chapter Sixteen

I WOULDN'T BE A very good content strategist if I didn't run through newsletter and social media strategies - don't give me that groan. I promise to make it as painless as possible. That being said, it does need to be done. Both of these need to be implemented in your business and now. Not only will this be yet another way to increase your following, showcase your abilities, and advertise in a cost-effective way, but you'll also be able to pull in sales from a dedicated audience. You'll be able to promote sales and share any launches you release. All to people who are excited to hear from you.

Let's start with your newsletter. This is probably one of the most important aspects of your business. Many business coaches, influencers, and top content producers constantly advocate using newsletters. They share their results and let you know they made six figures on the last launch and they <u>only</u> marketed the product to their email list. While this may cause you to roll your eyes, I want you to take a second and think about it.

Why build a newsletter? You've built a huge following on one social media platform or another and want to run your business off that channel. My question is: what is your business going to do should that social media platform go under or they shut your account down? Do you have a back-up plan? A place everyone's information is gathered and stored should anything like that happen?

No, of course you don't - unless you have an email list. Having this list is something which will prevent you from completely going out of business because of something out of your hands. It's how you protect your business. Not only are you actively making smart business choices, but you're building up a list of people who are your ultimate cheerleaders. A newsletter isn't an email you send out to people who automatically dump it in the trash. If that's happening, it's to purge your list or revamp your newsletter content.

People should only be on your list because they want to be there. Actively purging it and dumping people who don't open your emails or have multiple accounts may decrease your numbers, but it increases the strength of your list. You don't want anyone on your list who isn't dying to purchase your services or products as soon as you launch them. Remember, you own your email list - you get to decide who stays and who goes. It's time to get an email list created.

Whether you house your list in MailChimp, ConvertKit, or Mailerlite is up to you. It really doesn't matter what the "best" software is - it's what software works best for you and where your business is at right now. They all pretty much do the same things anyway, so you want to choose one you enjoy looking at and working in. It also helps if you can find resources to help you learn how to work it quickly.

Disclaimer: there are new laws put into existence about saving, sharing, and selling other people's information. For instance, the newest one which just went into effect is the General Data Protection Regulation (GDPR) law. This law is important to everyone, as you're building an online business. If even one European citizen signs up to your list and you don't adhere to the guidelines for the GDPR, you face **very** hefty fines. Take the time to research current newsletter/information laws in all countries.

Getting the newsletter set up isn't something you should worry about too much. It's all about what you're going to say to your list. The first email you send to them should be a welcome and thank you email. You want to show them you appreciate their support. The next five emails you send them afterwards should be value-filled. There shouldn't be any sales pitch, mention of your services, or inclusion of anything you offer. This gives your list time to get to know and trust you. It gives them so much value they'll want to dive deeper into certain topics.

The next email you send in this sequence, which should be number seven, is a soft offering. This means you're offering something free or potentially cheap. It is usually an email accompanied with tons of value and then makes a really subtle ask at the very end. This is what is called "soft-selling." I know this term makes it seem like a sleazy sales technique, but it's not. This is not to overwhelm or trick potential clients. You're offering them something they can afford (again, it's free or below $40) they have been asking for and want. You're offering them something with a ton of value, not just because you want to make a few bucks. You're focused on helping them. You're building a relationship with them. Not selling to them.

After your soft-selling seventh email, send another five-to-seven emails which are filled with value. This gets your list used to seeing you and further showcases your worth. It increases the chance of them buying something the next time you offer something. When you hit that next email (12th or 14th) in this segment, send a sales email which offers something a bit pricier or has a longer timeline. You can also reiterate what you offered in the first sales email, should they not want this higher-priced offer. This will probably lead to more sales of the lower-priced item, as your list knows you a bit better after all those emails.

Now what do you actually write in all of those emails? It's easy for me to say write a value-filled post. It's a whole different beast to actually write that type of post and be confident in doing so. It can be difficult to know whether what you have to say is valuable or not. To figure out if your readers need the information, ask questions:

- Is this helpful to my audience?
- Will this improve my audience's lives in any way?
- Is there action to take or a lesson to be learned from this?
- If my audience never read this, would it really matter?

Use the time you have when there are only a few people on your list as a testing period. Try out different layouts, use different graphics, and switch up how you address your list. Write in different styles, ask them for suggestions on what they want to learn from you, send out reader surveys. Having a small list is something to be grateful for and excited about. There are some amazing opportunities to play around while you have one. This is a great time to test out different options and work on creating the best newsletter you possibly can.

Enough rambling about newsletters. Let's move on to the social media portion of this chapter. You don't have to like social media. You can actually hate every part of it, but the fact of the matter is - you need it. It's vital for every small business. It's all about using it in the best way possible for your business. Sensing a theme? Everything you do needs to benefit you - nothing should be done just because somebody said you should or because it worked for someone else. Your business is not going to grow if you don't make it something you love and do only the things that work for where you are.

If your audience doesn't spend time in Facebook groups or hanging out on Snapchat, then you shouldn't be there. If your followers spend all of their time on YouTube, you better have a channel which produces consistent, valuable content for them to find. There isn't the option to interact with your audience in Pinterest so it shouldn't be where you spend a ton of time. Instagram has exploded into a hot bed of influencers and if your audience is on there and you can leverage those influencers, you should definitely be there.

This isn't news to you. You've heard this advice before because everyone tells you it's what you're supposed to do. You understand you "should" be posting multiple times a day. You get you "should" be developing a strategy for what to post and where to post. You understand you "should" be making social media a priority. You know you "should" get how to make this a seamless and easy process and yet have no idea where to start.

Social media is intense. It's a ton of work to keep up with and doesn't give a ton of reward for certain industries. Make it a little easier by creating a workflow. I'm going to give you an overview of how I created my social media workflow. If you're looking for a step-by-step walk through, Nora has a course in her Membership Hub. Check it out in the resource page. As she mentions, this workflow is not meant to replace or completely automate your social media. Checking in with your platforms and responding to comments and questions regularly will make your channels grow more than you ever know. You also want to interact with other accounts in order to increase your views.

Let's get this started, shall we? In order to set up a workflow to work for you, start by building up a content library. Take photos, download free images from a creative commons site like Creative Market, or purchase branded images from a photographer. Adhere to all copyright laws, but you need to start building up a library of content you can pull from. While the best option is to purchase branded photos, as long as you are adhering to copyright laws, any images will work. The images you are curating should be on brand. This means if you have a bright and colorful style, you shouldn't be saving photos with a "moody" vibe.

I realize not everyone has the budget to hire a photographer to take branded photos. If that's the case, I'd recommend taking the photos yourself. Use your smartphone, include plenty of light, and try out different angles. As a small business owner, I am liable for a lot of things. I don't want my business to be sued, then go under, while having to deal with legal issues and fees because I used an image I thought was part of the Creative Commons. The Creative Commons is a public copyright license which allows the free distribution of an otherwise copyrighted work. This lets the author give people the right to share, use, and build upon a work they created. I try to limit as much risk as I can, due to how feeble copyright law interpretations can be, and taking my own photos allows me to mitigate risk in this area.

Once you have your library stocked up with a few hundred photos, it's time to start creating. The images need to be paired with text. Your library needs to be put to good use. Collect quotes and pair them with relevant photos. Create two-to-five captions for Twitter for every blog post you've created. Pair those up with relevant images. Create captions for every offer or product you have available. Pair those captions with relevant images in your library. Write captions on lessons you've learned in your life. Pull stories and experiences you've been through and write some text on that. See how easy this is?

You don't want to have to do hours of research trying to find one image for one quote or caption. You want to do maybe ten minutes of scrolling in your image library and be able to pick a photo which is on brand. This will save you time and effort. Along the same vein of saving time and effort, I'd also suggest creating several lists of vital information you probably search for and use regularly without even knowing it. Hashtags you use, guest post links, affiliate links, and all your social media links are all great lists to create and store.

Once you have your library set up and have written out all of your captions, you can start to schedule it all out in your social media scheduler. As you know, I've used CoSchedule and Buffer, but you can use any of the software we talked about back in Chapter 5. Since you've already gone through the chapter about all of these tools, I assume you've already gotten your accounts and are on your way to setting up a workflow for dealing with all of them.

Social media isn't a hard concept. It's not something you should be freaking out about or even spending too much time doing. Once your social media library is set up, you never have to set it up again. You keep adding to and updating it with all of the new content you create. You'll never have to spend an exorbitant amount of time building a content well like this. Not only will creating this library and workflow allow you to feel good about posting on social media and eliminate your frustrations, but it will result in a tailored and loyal community which will turn into some amazing clients for your business!

Ebooks, Videos, and Other Upgrades

Chapter Seventeen

AFTER BUILDING UP YOUR blog content, preparing your newsletter, and getting your social media channels on track, it's time to start offering even more value. A ton of people will protest this chapter. Their arguments range from "I don't want to give away everything for free" to "why provide value to people other than my current clients?" They are coming at this all wrong. They are focused on this issue with a fixed mindset. We want to focus on it with a growth mindset.

Value is today's global currency. It's the only way people truly start to trust and believe you. Not only do content upgrades allow you to provide the necessary value, but they also bring more traffic. Content upgrades help pinpoint more pings a search engine is looking for and boosts the posts you published. It's also more appealing for your audience to share with their network and community. They get to be the one to introduce a knowledgeable, valuable, and helpful expert to their friends. Not to mention, it's a great way to increase your newsletter subscribers and bring in loyal audience members.

I know when I was first starting out, I got a ton of advice to add content upgrades to all of my blog posts in order to build up my email. It sounded simple, was an easy concept to understand, and I was excited to get started. I got ideas brainstormed, outlined some stuff, and then stalled - I can't design. I barely know how to open up a design software, let alone the right one. How the heck was I supposed to figure this out? I didn't want to have to learn Adobe InDesign or Photoshop or anything like that. I wanted it simple.

How did I end up making content upgrades my community enjoyed and actually used? I made some without any thought as to what my community would like or why. I was under so much pressure to make a perfect upgrade document for them, I was stifling myself and my creativity. I had to take a step back and just create something for the sake of creating it. I then went back and spruced it up a bit. I used my favorite tool, Canva, to create a simple, yet clean design. I uploaded the file onto SquareSpace's file storage and linked it to my email list software.

Content upgrades are one of the easiest parts of creating content. The reason being is the content upgrade topics are an extension of the article, a worksheet to help your community work through the topic, or a dive deeper into the topic in a podcast or video format. The upgrade should be in whatever format works for you and the topic. This upgrade needs to be useful and something your audience wants. You can't create a list of the different breeds of dogs when you're a freelance copywriter. Why would your audience want that? A one-page document with five simple tips to become a better writer is something they might want.

The term content upgrade means you're upgrading your content's value. You're literally adding extra value to help your audience better understand or interact with your content. Always give more than you take. Creating these upgrades will always benefit you. There is no draw back to providing more help to your audience, even if they never become a client. It gives you a great talking point and allows you the opportunity to showcase more of your skills. Plus, once someone uses one of your upgrades and their life improves, you have a lifelong cheerleader. They will shout your praises from the roof - or the street, whichever is safer.

Creating these upgrades isn't as hard as you think. In order to write an ebook, come up with a topic, create an outline for what you want to cover, and then start writing! Once you've finished writing, edit the book. Read through it a couple of times. Send it to a couple of your friends or business buddies. Then, format and create a cover for it. Use the tips and strategies I've given you along the way to market it. There you have it - a completed ebook. Remember, they don't need to be long - I've seen some as small as four pages, with one page as a cover and a second page as the biography and business information page. This doesn't have to take forever and be this big difficult task on your to-do list; it needs to cover the topic as completely as possible - that's all.

To create videos, you will need some device which records and some type of microphone. Using your smartphone and headphones with a microphone is perfectly acceptable at the beginning. Your videos don't need to be perfect when you're starting out. One of my favorite quotes which illustrates this vividly is by Reid Hoffman, "If you're not embarrassed by the first version of your product, you've launched too late." This is what I keep in mind if I ever start down the comparison path. If you have more advanced equipment, great - use it.

These methods can be used for just about every type of content upgrade. You brainstorm some ideas, create an outline, create a script or write a few key points, and then make it! Once you've finished, edit it, format it, and create a cover. Graphics are made in Canva. See how easy this process can be? Once it's been edited and all the graphics have been added, include it in your email funnel and start ranking in followers.

Creating content upgrades should be something you do because you enjoy them. If you hate doing them, then don't create them. I promise you, it is so much better to not create something you hate then it is to create it terribly. The benefits associated with content upgrades won't come to you in anywhere near as close as everyone has been promising if you hate it. You'll end up mad at it for failing and frustrated you spent so much time making something you didn't even like in the first place. You'll resent it, never publish it, and forever bash on the use of content upgrades, never wanting to download one yourself, ever again.

Ok, I might be getting a bit dramatic, but you know what I'm saying.

You should never create something just because someone said you should. If you try creating it and it doesn't resonate with you, dump it. If you need more help, ask for it. Do what works best for you and your business. I promise following every single "should" you've been given will do nothing to get your business where you had hoped. The only way to get your business where you want it to be is to follow your intuition and do what feels good for you.

Content Hoarders Anonymous

Content Hoarders Anonymous

YOU'RE A BUSINESS OWNER. You've become comfortable with identifying yourself as one. You're excited about what it means for you and for your business as a whole. You can't wait to see how it changes your entire life. You start to consume articles and videos which tell you what you "should" be doing. You download document after document in order to learn more or use a different method you're hoping will click.

You're focused on finding the "best" method, learning everything you can, and not missing out.

All the experts say you should never stop learning. You took this advice to heart and spend your time learning as much as you can. You end up in a stalemate in business. You spend all of your time consuming content other people have published. You end up forgetting to create your own content. "Business time" is essentially you consuming, downloading, and taking notes you'll never look back on or read through. You don't have any clients, you aren't making any money, and you're constantly overworked and stressed out because you can't keep up with all of the content.

If you're surprised at how accurately this paints a picture of your life, don't be. I spent an entire year feeling like this. My "work" time consisted of consuming as much as I could, while my downtime consisted of finding more content to consume. I would snap at my boyfriend (now, fiancé) to let me work because I was always busy. I would spend my time consumed with thoughts about all of the work I had to do, because there was no way I could leave all of those worksheets empty. It was a nasty, overwhelming, and completely useless time in my life.

Consuming tons of the same type of content

didn't increase my skills, my knowledge, or my confidence. In fact, it actually lowered my confidence levels. I kept reviewed the same topics over and over. It made me wonder if I actually knew what I was talking about and if I was educated enough to be able to charge for my skills. I questioned everything I knew and what I thought I didn't know. I was so worried about missing out on vital information, I convinced myself the information I had wasn't valuable or important enough. Consuming too much content was my way of productively procrastinating - putting off the work I needed to be doing by accomplishing something else of little to no value.

Content hoarding is real. It's a result of fear. It can be the fear of success, failure, bad clients, good clients, being "found out," and so many more. It can be as simple as trying to get your social media content created and the fear of overwhelm it causes or as complex as the fear of having money to burn in your bank account. I found figuring out *why* I wanted to download, hoard, and consume other people's content helped me to sort through my emotions and stop signing up for so much. I asked myself what I was afraid of, why I thought *these* downloads were different, how *these* downloads were going to change my life.

After discovering I was afraid of taking on the responsibility of a client, feared success and what that meant for me, and feared I didn't have the right knowledge to help my clients in any way, I took action. I went through my house, my bags, and my car and gathered everything I had into one pile in one location. I had the ability to see exactly how much I actually had downloaded. I was shocked by the shear amount of useless downloads I had hoarded in and around me. I had four 3" binders full of documents, worksheets, ebooks, and so much more. My mind and workspace were severely cluttered and it wasn't just affecting my ability to focus, but also my creativity and my confidence.

However, all of the downloads I signed up for were amazingly well designed and had some inspiring information. Every business owner put a lot of time in on these amazing content upgrades and I'm sure they were vital to many people's success. They just weren't helpful or useful to me. They did more harm than good. Realizing this allowed me to not feel as guilty for deleting and throwing away all of these downloads. I had to acknowledge the fact I was being buried under trying to keep and fill out every single download I had. I had absolutely no business and yet was incredibly busy "working!" I had to face the fact I didn't need these worksheets - in fact, I needed these worksheets to be gone.

I spent my entire first year of business consuming anything and everything I could get my hands on. I didn't realize why I wasn't making money at first. I ended up taking a step back from my business for six months before I realized what was holding me back. I unsubscribed, threw away, and deleted a ton of information. After getting rid of the majority of the content I was obsessed with consuming, I was able to focus on creating content. Creating content is so important because it is what your potential clients use to gauge how knowledgeable you are about your craft. It's what gets you in front of your audience and is what you use to market your business. Without content, there's nothing for you to share. There's no way for you to grow.

Focusing your efforts and energy on creating your own content keeps you from spinning your wheels downloading other content. You don't want to get caught in the same cycle I did - downloading every piece you see and hoarding everything. I think the worst part of the year was feeling so overwhelmed. I didn't even have any clients and yet I had created so much "work" for myself I couldn't handle it. Take the necessary steps to realign your focus, making sure you're creating more content than you consume. If you need to, take a step back from social media.

The next time you find yourself about to download yet another opt-in from a blog post, ask yourself if it's relevant. Ask if it's necessary. Ask how your life or business is going to change after you go through this document. Ask if it can actually help your life. Ask why this download is important. Most importantly, ask if you're actually going to take the time to fill out the worksheet and then implement the ideas and action items it presents.

Most of you will probably answer no or not really to many of these questions. If you have stacks of downloads filling your desk, filing cabinet, or bookmarks, you need to back away from that new download you think you have to have. Back away from the blog posts, video, or new course. Don't even think about subscribing to that newsletter - I don't care how great other people say the content is. Don't even think about signing up for another webinar - I don't care if there is information you just have to have. Do not click on another download. I don't care if your computer auto populates your information into the necessary fields. Delete it all and back away.

You don't need another download. You don't need to fill your online storages with tons of worksheets and checklists. You don't need to gain the information a one-page worksheet is going to give you. You need to take action and get your business growing. It's time to stop consuming and start producing. The only way your business is going to grow is by publishing consistent content. The only way you can publish anything is if you take action and start creating. Stop focusing on consuming and start creating.

It can be hard to quit downloading content. I know you think you can stop at any time. I know it seems like something people don't even need to worry about. I felt the same way. It was a wake up call when I looked up and finally realized I had wasted a year downloading and consuming. My eyes were open to what an issue content hoarding can actually be. I spent my next year doing as much action as I could and not letting myself download anything new.

After discovering what was holding me back from making money, I am proud to say I ended my second year with just over $3,000 made. I am on track to earn even more in the coming years. None of it was consistent, I had a hard time earning it, and I kept falling back into the rabbit hole of consuming more times than I could count, but I made progress. I created. I took action. I moved forward. That's all I could ask for.

I'm sure a ton of people's response to this chapter is going to be "But Kaylee, what do I do when I don't know anything about a certain subject or need the information on the download?" Well, here's the thing: if it's of a subject you don't know about, there's a few things to consider. Do you need to know this subject right now? Unless you have a client who is paying you for this subject, then no, you don't need to know it. Learning on the job is the best way for you to gain the skills necessary and leave all of the fluff out. Why do you need this information? Is it going to change your life in any way? Is it going to help you improve yourself? If you can't answer these questions in a way which doesn't sound like you're making excuses, then you're just lying to yourself.

Disclaimer: I am in no way advocating for you to sell services you know nothing about. You should be providing valuable services.

It's time to stop consuming so much. You need to take action on your dreams. I suggest you start by taking a look at your mindset and figuring out what you're so afraid of. I realized I was consuming so much because I was afraid of actually shouldering any responsibility to make a client happy. Why are you so afraid to actually work with clients? Taking action is the only way you're going to overcome these mindset issues. It's the only way you'll be able to make your dreams come true. What are you going to do?

Diving into your mindset will allow you to get passed blocks you didn't know you had. It will allow you to improve your life and make more money than you ever believed. It will change your entire life. Mindset is the key to your dreams.

KAYLEE WHITE

My Overwhelm Kit

Chapter Nineteen

BUILDING A BUSINESS IS overwhelming. We've been over setting up our business, dealing with content consumption, getting our goals and content strategies set up, finding your passion, determining the tools, software, and style you'll use, budgeting your whole venture, building your website, and getting a CRM in place. I'm sure you're facing a ton of decision-fatigue and are overwhelmed with everything you have to get done.

This is completely normal! I don't want you believing I did all of this in a manner of a weeks or even months. This took me years to nail down. That being said, don't be discouraged! My path looks completely different from what yours is going to look like. Your path may be much shorter than mine. The most important thing to remember is this: beyond standard business sales techniques and typical customer service practices your consumers expect, you really don't "have" to do much of anything. Don't like webinars? Don't do them! Don't want to write? Don't have a blog. These are practices which help your business in many ways. They are not, however, vital pieces of the success puzzle.

Take your time to figure out what works best for you and your business. If you don't love aspects of what you do, then change it, delegate it, and figure out how to make it something you might enjoy. If you don't, the work you're doing becomes something you dread waking up and doing. You're not doing all this work to build a business you dread. Do what feels good to you and your audience.

When I start feeling overwhelmed, there are several things I do to combat it. The first thing I do is get a list going. I write out every single item I need to accomplish. This isn't a list for just business items. This is an exhaustive list for everything I need to get done. Once I have everything written down, I determine five priority tasks I want to accomplish within the next day, week, or month - depending on how much work needs to go into each of them. I do this by going through each task and determining which have deadlines. Those are tasks I need to accomplish first. I work on them in the order of deadline coming up.

After these tasks have been completed or have been worked on enough to move me to the next task, I move onto other tasks which may not have a specific deadline attached. The other thing I keep in mind is this list doesn't need to be all finished in a single day. I need to take it one day at a time. This means I need to get a schedule going for the day. Realistically, what am I going to be able to accomplish during this day?

Keeping this thought in mind, I do what I can. I set my intention for each day and do what I need to do. If at the end of this book, you've got a plan in place to tackle all of these tasks, my job is done. You should feel proud of getting there, not disappointed you weren't perfect and completed it all in a day. The information in this book is all useful, necessary, and needed. It's not going anywhere. It's always here should you need to refer back to it, so don't pressure yourself into attempting to complete everything in an unrealistic timeline.

That being said, please don't put all of this off. Just because you don't have to complete all of this in a day doesn't mean you can put the whole thing off indefinitely. List out everything you need to accomplish and then get it scheduled. I have a task list of all of the action items we've gone over at the back of the book so you have an easy access guide as to what you should be doing. Regardless of if it's in a Google Calendar, physical planner, or project management software like Trello or Asana, there needs to be a due date assigned to each task.

Now, should you feel overwhelmed or anxiety hit you, there are several things you can do to combat it. This is when you start breaking out into a fantastic dance party, take a walk through a park, change your setting, delegate tasks out, write in a journal, debrief weekly with a close friend or do whatever you can to get your mind off of those feelings. Take time for self-care. Take care of yourself. Spend time relaxing. When you're overwhelmed, it's your body's way of telling you it's time for a break.

Sometimes, no matter what you plan or do, the feeling of overwhelm still persists. No matter what you do, you can't shake the feeling. It sucks. It isn't fun and it feels like you can never shake it. I have had several times where I legitimately thought I would be overwhelmed for the rest of my life. Remember the meme of the guy sitting in hell saying, "This is fine." That's what it felt like.

I'm here to tell your mind can be a bit of a jerk. It helps to remember "this too shall pass." Nothing lasts forever. Not even all of the negative feelings and circumstances you believe plague your life. You need to keep your mindset in check if you are to succeed without feeling like you're going to break down at any moment. One of the mantras I keep at the forefront of my mind is something Jen Sincero described perfectly in her book, "You Are A Badass." She said, "Our thoughts become our words, our words become beliefs, our beliefs become our actions, our actions become our habits, and our habits become our realities."

It's time to stop struggling against how you're feeling. It's time to develop some techniques and practices to help you work throughout these feelings. For me, when I get overwhelmed, I turn on a Harry Potter movie or grab a good book and spend some time away. When I come back to my work, I start with a list. (If you haven't noticed, I love my lists.) From there, I assign dates, get a schedule set up, and then figure out what three tasks I can accomplish that day. What can you do to combat overwhelm?

Building Your Team

Chapter Twenty

I'M GOING TO BE completely honest with you. I'm not ready for this step. I want to be. I'm really excited for the time in my business where I can build a team of people who are motivated and ready to take on the world with me.

That aside, I'm not ready to go there. I decided to keep this chapter in the book because some of you are ready. Some of you don't know if you're ready. Others have no idea how to even think about this type of stuff. This chapter is a brief introduction to figuring out this part of your business.

Ashley Mackey Cox, the founder and owner of SproutHR, is not only amazing at helping you navigate the scary waters of dealing with human resources and laws, but she is also one of the nicest people you'll ever meet. She has worked with the likes of Kroger and J. Crew so when she says something, you better listen up.

If you are in a position to start hiring, first off, congratulations! That's a big step and an amazing accomplishment. Second, read Ashley's article on "How to Know When to Hire a Pro vs. A Newbie" which is linked on our resources page. This helps you narrow down your search parameters. Not only will you learn more about what you're going to want out of your new team member, but you're also going to know where to start looking for them.

When you start thinking about and preparing to grow a team, instead of jumping in, you will save yourself so much time and money. You won't rush into hiring someone who doesn't quite fit well with the culture you want to create, as well as the idea of what you wanted them to handle. You won't waste the money of creating workflows and on-boarding this new member with emails, access to your other tools and more. Plus, you don't have the headache of fixing relationships with vendors or clients they may have messed up.

When you get clear on what you're wanting and needing, you are able to make the whole process run smoother and avoid wasting time and money. I suggest spending some time going over another blog post Ashley published called "Who Should I Hire First? | Determining Your Needs vs. Wants," also linked to our resources page. In this blog post, Ashley details out the first steps to figuring out how to hire your first team member. She created a full on series to help you, but this is the first post I'd start with.

Hiring someone to join your team is such a wonderful step in your business. You've gotten to a point where you can simplify your life immensely. The only problem is if you don't prepare for it correctly and have a plan in place, you could also complicate your life more than when you were doing everything yourself. Don't add another layer of complication. Take time to get prepared and have a plan.

Once you have your plan, you can start getting things off your plate. Have a ton of calls to schedule for follow-ups? Have your team member do it. Need to get a ton of research done for potential clients or a client project? Delegate it out. Have a list of projects you've been wanting to get done for forever? Send it to this new employee and get it done!

Once you have a plan together, start making it work. Put together systems, write out your processes for certain parts of your business, and document everything. Get all of these systems and procedures figured out, before you hire someone.

When it comes to hiring your first team member, you have to keep in mind you aren't bringing them on as a status symbol. They are there to make your life easier. They are taking on this role as a source of income. While it's important to find someone who believes what you're providing is necessary, they will never care about your business as much as you do. You need to find someone who fits well with what you are trying to accomplish and will do good work for your business.

Hiring someone is all about expanding your business. They need to be able to take on projects and tasks so you are able to move on and find money-making tasks to incorporate and complete. You shouldn't be stuck babysitting your team member.

Remember, you're building a team, not hiring employees to work at Dunder Mifflin. The goal of hiring your first team member is to help you. Don't rush into this decision too fast. There's a process and it will benefit you to follow it.

Cold Pitching vs. Job Boards

Chapter Twenty-One

I'M GOING TO BE honest, choosing the path you're going to take to find clients is really confusing. The debate between cold pitching and using job boards has been going on for years. Not only have both sides been constantly debating which method is more viable for growing your business, but each side has some incredibly valid points. There is no right or wrong direction. There is a right or wrong way for you. So pay attention and spend some time thinking about which method is right for you.

I'm going to start this discussion with job boards. There are a lot of people who absolutely love them. They swear by them and make good money from them. They've learned the system and are good at playing it to their advantage. These job boards provide them their living.

The other side are people who fiercely and passionately loath job boards. Not only do they believe a living can't be made through job boards, but they also believe it is ruining the industry. They claim having freelancers accept jobs at such low price points, as are typical for job boards, brings the entire industry down. The argument is the fact clients start believing the job board prices are actually industry standard.

I'm not going to tell you whether I believe one side or the other. Why? I actually believe them both. There really is no one - size fits all formula. The best part is you don't really need to choose one path or the other. In fact, it's advisable you don't choose just one path. Remember, you don't want all your eggs in one basket. That's not a sound business practice.

There are several options you have in order to create the best chance of success for your business. The way to find out what works for you is through trial and error. My process is deeply modeled after my favorite people ever: Jenny and Alex. Check out my process below.

I focus mostly on cold pitching to potential clients. While I work on this process, I am "schmoozing" local business owners at local networking events. I'm speaking and engaging with them, building relationships. On top of all of this, I have two methods for finding more clients: I have a couple referral partners and I use job boards.

I want to be clear: this method or system or whatever you want to call it for gaining clients and growing my business was all Jenny and Alex's idea. Do you see how brilliant they are? I envy their friends because all I want to do is hang out with them all day, soaking up their amazing knowledge.

Let me break this down a little further so you understand. I cold pitch businesses I love and am excited about with emails. I am connecting with and talking to CEO's of businesses I love on LinkedIn. I develop relationships with these CEO's and get to know them. When they're looking to get content written, they think of me because I've formed a relationship with them!

I constantly check reputable job boards -

LinkedIn, for example - and send off tailored email pitches to them. In this way, I'm approaching companies who are looking for a copywriter, without actually applying for a job I don't want. I send the tailored emails full of value and benefits of hiring a freelancer versus hiring a full-time employee to the people posting these job postings and find projects this way.

The last method I use to find clients is through referral partners. Referral partners are people who are in industries which end up working regularly with my ideal clients. These are people who are graphic designers, web developers, branding coaches, and more. These people regularly work with clients to set up a portion of their business and then need to refer them to someone else who can write for them. I developed relationships with these business owners and referred clients back and forth.

These are all methods I use to find clients. I participate in each method equally. When I find one method slows down, I focus on another. I always have potential clients brewing in each of these methods and am working to build my contacts as much as possible. The key to building successful client pipelines is the follow-up. Regardless which methods work for you, following-up is the key to your success.

Managing Clients

Chapter Twenty-Two

CLIENTS ARE YOUR BUSINESS'S life line. They give you leverage to accomplish all of your goals and dreams. When it comes to dealing with clients, there are several things you need to keep in mind. Every client is different. The way they work, how they process information, and their personalities are all on different parts of a spectrum. Some of them will be dreams, others will be nightmares. You need to be prepared for all sorts of amazing, horrible, and just plain boggling things to happen while you're working with clients.

Being a freelancer, you're able to pick and choose which clients you want to work with. You don't have to take on every client you speak with. That being said, we all go through the horrible client process because we need the money, experience, and feel like we have no other choice. As a business owner, you have every choice of who you take on as a client. Taking on a dream client can be amazing and make you feel like every single horrible thing you've gone through is worth it. It just takes a keen eye to flush out which clients are dreams and which are nightmares. Keep a list of red flags from any negative experiences you or other people you know have gone through to reference.

The fun part of working with clients comes when you're freelancing on the side. If you're doing this while you're still in school or have a full-time job, you have a lot more to contend with. You have to be very intentional about what you do and when you do it. I have divided up this chapter into three sections: School, Day Job, and Full-Time. I am going to give you some tips on managing clients no matter which stage you're in.

Disclaimer: I am not a mom, so I felt it best not to speak on this topic. I have gone through the experiences talked about below. I know what it all feels like. That being said, these tips worked for me. Feel free to adapt them to your own situation.

School

When you're in school and trying to manage clients, you have to remember something - school has to come first. I know all of the programs and courses you've been hoarding and binge-taking gets you motivated and makes you feel like you'll never need to take another class or hold down a real job. I know how you feel. Jenny and Alex make me truly believe I can take on the world. Every time I hear one of these girls talk, I want to quit my job right there and then!

    The thing is, school is important. It has to be your priority while you're in it. At the very minimum, you need a high school degree. You need to have the basics of school done. Our world is very unforgiving if you haven't at least finished high school. If you're in college, that's a whole different story. While I believe everyone should at least earn their Associate's Degree, I understand college isn't for everyone and thankfully, no higher education is required to be a freelancer.

If you're in school, focus on school. I know you want to build your business and be available at all times for your clients, but you can't. You have other commitments. This by no means should result in bad customer service. You want to make sure you're taking care of your clients, even if you can't be available to them as much as you'd like.

There are ways you can counteract all of this. The first thing you want to do is set expectations. Let your clients know you are still in school and have restricted hours of access. If you have the ability to, set up some office hours. This could mean you're available by email, phone, or both during certain hours on certain days. If possible, set aside a two-hour window each day where you can answer questions and address concerns.

Managing clients while in school is all about being intentional with your time. As long as you communicate what you're circumstances are, manage expectations, constantly communicate with your clients, and do your best, you'll manage just fine.

Day Job

Managing clients while holding down a full-time job is tough. It's not any easier because you finished school. It's still handling clients. You still need to deal with different personalities, manage expectations, and complete the services you've sold. There is one big difference.

You have more time. For most of us, when we leave work, we're done. We get home and cook dinner, do maybe ten minutes of cleaning, and then watch like five or six hours of television. Then, when asked about the progress we've made on the projects we keep talking about, we get defensive and say we've been SO busy. The truth is we get so sidetracked by our day-to-day routines that we forget about our dreams.

It's time to set aside these distractions. It's time to make your dreams come true. You have absolutely no excuse. Remember this is all about tough love. You don't have homework, you don't need to study, and you don't have to work on group projects (let me tell you, I hated those with a fiery passion).

You don't need to split your time between class, everything class required, and managing clients. You go to work, you come home, and you get to work. There is no time to be messing around. You are building a business here. You are working to shape your future. Stop dismissing it like it's last week's laundry you still haven't put up and get serious.

Using the time you have, you can create all the

content and business you will ever need. You can start waking up earlier. You can start giving up your TV time. You can get organized and start completing tasks in a bulk fashion. Complaining you don't have the time to make your dreams come true is a lie you're using as an excuse not to feel uncomfortable.

Finish all of your client work during your free time. Hold phone calls and meetings with potential and current clients during your lunch hours and before work. Create systems and workflows to allow you to be as efficient as possible.

All of this is totally doable. It isn't brain surgery. All you need to do is get organized. You need to create a system for what you do and how you do it. Now is not the time to focus on being perfect. You need to be focused on staying organized and keeping on top of everything.

Full-Time

While you may have the ability to work on your business full-time, you still have to be focused and create workflows to keep everything in line. Running a business pulls your focus in several different directions, not to mention our own tendency to procrastinate and put our focus on unimportant things.

The best part of being a full-time freelancer is you literally decide what you want to focus on. You get to do what you want and focus your attention on what you want. You decided you don't want to be on Pinterest? Don't focus on it. You decided you don't want to have a blog? You don't have to deal with one. You get to make those kinds of decisions without having to defend them to anybody. They just need to make sense for your business.

The perks of being a full-time freelancer can also be your downfall. If you don't make sure you have some sort of schedule set up, you'll never get anything done. You want to make sure you know what you need to accomplish for every single part of your business. This means every single social media post on every single platform you've decided to be on, every blog post, all of your client work, every task you need for client acquisition, any bookkeeping tasks, keeping up-to-date on new market trends, and so much more.

With more time to focus on your business, you really have to get intentional about what you're going to work on. If you don't curtail this now, you'll end up with several months wasted on trying to keep up with meaningless tasks and things which have no real importance to your business as a whole. You'll probably end up focusing more on social media and blogging instead of pitching or scouring job boards because you weren't paying attention to how much time you spent on social media.

Intention will help you set expectations and get a reasonable schedule set up so you know what you need to do. There's no guessing. You don't need to figure out how you want to work each day. You know what you need to do and how to do it. You know how to get what you want and what you need to get done. Knowing what your intention is each day gives you this knowledge, because you know what you're working towards.

While having the freedom of being your own boss comes with some amazing advantages, it takes a focused mind and a well-thought out plan to make it work. Don't be discouraged if you think of yourself as unfocused and unorganized. This line of thought comes from having mindset blocks. You're able to learn the skills needed to become focused. People aren't just born with it - you can learn it too. It comes from practice. Your success is all your own. Your failure is all on you. You have all of the power in your hands. It's up to you.

Planning the Event of a Lifetime

Chapter Twenty-Three

BY THIS TIME, YOU'RE probably feeling like a professional at all of this. You've learned a lot. We've had a good time and while we still have some time together, we are getting to the end. There are some things you should remember:

- Always celebrate the small wins.

- Be grateful for the clients who teach you how to stand up for yourself.
- Don't put so much pressure on yourself.
- Enjoy every step of the journey - even the crappy ones.
- Make the leap. Try something new.

I realize every single one of these is a cliche everyone tells you. However, there is a phrase I'm especially partial to. While this saying may not be wholly original, it is a saying which has gotten me through many tough times throughout my life and career. It comes in two small statements:

There is always hope.
Everything is going to be fine.

Depending on the situation, I use one or both of these phrases. They have gotten me through heartbreaks, panic attacks, almost failing out of college, getting let go from a job I was way too invested in, and so much more. I know things can seem impossible, but using these phrases has pulled me through every situation. Not only do I constantly repeat them, but I actually believe every single word.

There is <u>always</u> hope.

<u>Everything</u> is going to be fine.

This all comes because I really want you to trust yourself throughout this whole process. Life isn't easy, but you can get through this. I know you can create the business and life of your dreams. It just takes a little bit of muscle and stubbornness. Never give up.

As sappy as those few pages were, it's time to pump up the excitement a bit. It's time to plan the event of the lifetime. I know this may freak out my fellow introverts and drive all extroverts to focus only on this event, instead of their business, but hold on. This is not supposed to a big thing - unless you want it to be. The event of the season is meant to be a celebration for you. Don't make this into something else for you to do. Don't make this into a to-do list item for you to freak out over.

This can literally be a day you take to celebrate yourself. Do a spa day, spend a day being completely lazy, and avoid all responsibility for a day. This is not supposed to be something you stress yourself out over. You want this "event of a lifetime" to feel fun and celebrate how hard you've worked to get to where you are. It needs to be something you look forward to and are excited about. Remember, this is your event - there are no requirements nor expectations for how it's supposed to look or what you're supposed to do.

Should you be feeling a bit more energetic and celebratory, then throw a gathering. Get all of your friends and family together and host a thank you party. Use this time to thank each and every person for supporting you, believing in you, and being there for you. Share your vision for how you're going to move forward and how all of your loved ones can help and support you.

This event isn't meant for you to brag about your success or rub it in your friends and family' faces. It's meant to celebrate a milestone, a success, and your business as a whole. It's meant to celebrate every single person who has helped you along the way. It takes a village to achieve success. Use this to thank everyone. It can be such a confidence boost to focus on the little and big successes you've achieved. You're a business owner. This event is meant to celebrate everything you have accomplished and are working toward.

If you don't want the attention, turn this into a customer appreciation event. Invite members of your local business community and have a networking event or a BYOB - Bring Your Own Beer party everybody is invited to. This is a great way to build a larger network and grow your local community. This is a win-win; you can celebrate your business and grow your business relationships at the same time.

I swear planning this event and putting all of this together is totally worth going through. Not only will you feel rejuvenated and ready to take on up-leveling your business, you will develop some amazing relationships and get closer to the ones you already have. Hosting this event, regardless of the form, allows your support network to express their pride and support for you. It gives them a chance to tell you exactly what they think of you and what you're doing.

To actually plan the event, it doesn't have to be anything huge. Grab some platters of food, some of your marketing materials, and a location and you're good to go! This event is meant to focus on you, your business, and the people there. You don't need - and shouldn't even entertain the idea of doing - some big presentation. Nobody wants to sit through that and you shouldn't be stressing about making it.

This is meant to be a fun, celebratory event. Don't force your guests to sit through another Power-Point slideshow. You don't care about those - why should they? Now stop fussing over useless corporate practices and go enjoy yourself. You deserve it, business owner!

HOW NOT TO BE JUST ANOTHER
                  FREELANCER

Mindset

Chapter Twenty-Four

THIS IS WITHOUT A doubt THE most important chapter in this entire book. Do not skip or skim this chapter. If you have a bit of free time or are generally feeling a bit off, read this chapter. When you finish this chapter, read it again. I'm serious. It doesn't matter what is going on in your life. This chapter is full of incredibly important information you can and should use to create the best life you can.

If I had to share my number one tool for business success, it would be mindset. The importance and benefits of doing mindset work cannot be overstated. Seriously, I will argue having the right mindset is the difference between having a six-figure business and not having a business at all. I know what you're thinking, "why is it one of the last chapters in the book?" I'll tell you why - because you weren't ready for it. The journey we've taken to get you here has been a long one. It is a necessary one. It is one you should be immensely proud of, but it had to be taken before you could get to this point.

Since you've gotten this far in your journey, I really need you to focus. This isn't going to be easy. Improving, shifting, and changing your mindset is not a walk in the park. This is not to say it's impossible. Improving and changing your mindset is just as hard or as easy as you believe it to be. If you come into this chapter thinking this is going to be a long, difficult road, then it will be. If you read this chapter thinking how much fun this is going to be and how you can't wait to see where you end up, then it's going to be a fun and easy thing to do.

Disclaimer: While mindset work doesn't have to be hard, things will not always happen immediately. We can't predict or make anything "happen" for us. We have to keep on doing the consistent mindset work, whether something happens or not.

Improving your mindset is all about asking yourself questions. It's a way to challenge your beliefs and create new ones. Why do you feel a certain way? What made you say you can't do it? Who has lead you to believe being successful is hard work? You want to question everything. To get started, set aside 30 minutes a day to work on your mindset. Once it becomes a solidified habit, bump up the time to a full hour. If you ever feel extra, schedule a day where you do mindset work for four-to-five hours.

Mindset work can take on several different forms. There's the always faithful journaling, going to counseling, drawing, coloring in coloring books, or walking. Any mindful activity which requires you to think or feel and helps you go deeper into yourself can be considered mindset work. There's also this amazing new technique Alex taught the members of the Six-Figure Freelancer Academy called the Just Sit There Diet (JST). The Just Sit There Diet is literally just sitting there. You want to sit in as much silence as possible.

The Just Sit There Diet is different from meditating because you are not trying to clear your mind or even focus on one thing. You want your thoughts to run free until you hit on one you can really pick apart. Say you have the thought "Man, it's really difficult for me to sit in silence doing absolutely nothing for a full hour." This is a perfect time to figure out why you believe that. Why do you believe it's difficult? Does it have to be difficult? What can you do to make it easier?

Mindset work is going to make you uncomfortable because it's changing your core beliefs.

You're going to be fidgety and want to procrastinate doing it. This is because it is getting you closer to everything you've ever wanted. Your brain is freaking out about that! It doesn't want to change. It doesn't care about your success, it's focused on your survival. That's all it cares about. That's all it will do. So everything it does, everything it thinks, everything it makes you do is all an effect of your brain wanting you to survive. Which is nice and all, but keeps you from going after your dreams, no matter how much you want them.

My biggest realization from regularly doing mindset work is learning I was living my life with a fixed mindset. This meant I avoided wanting to stretch myself, doing new things, and felt dumb unless I was praised or sure I was better than someone else. I never raised my hand unless I was absolutely sure of the answer. I never wanted to open myself up to new experiences because I thought I'd look foolish or get made fun of. As a 25-year-old woman, this sounds ridiculous when written or said out loud.

The good news about having a fixed mindset is it can be changed. I'm not stuck with this mindset. In other words, it's not as "fixed" as it may seem. I can challenge the beliefs I hold and work to move my mindset towards growth. I can put myself in situations which test my skills, use tools to reflect on my experiences, and be intentional about having a growth mindset. While it will always be natural for me to want to sit on the sidelines and avoid growing, I can develop habits which allow me to move into a growth mindset. I can incorporate additional actions and activities into my routine to keep my mind from slipping into a fixed mindset.

While doing mindset work can seem vague and utterly frustrating - seriously, I still get so frustrated - you must continue forward. You need to do at least an hour's worth of mindset work a day. The benefits this can have on your business are too massive to ignore. Improving your mindset and changing your belief even a micro-millimeter can literally bring in thousands more dollars. As an example, changing the belief you can only work with certain types of businesses who have a certain level of success can literally bring in thousands of dollars.

Changing your beliefs from "I can't work with any of the big dogs" to "I know how to wow every single prospective client and become the business owner I want to be" can open up your entire world and allow you to work with some serious dream clients.

Changing your mindset, improving your beliefs, and focusing on believing in yourself are all actions you can do to improve your business. It is all about improving your skills in a way which makes you confident and moves you into the role of an expert. Seriously, working on your mindset each and every day should be your number one priority. If possible, you should be doing it as soon as you wake up. Make the decision right now to never go to bed without completing your mindset practice. This isn't a joke. This is something you *never* skip. Your dream life is attainable, but only if you're willing to commit to it.

When you've decided to fully commit to doing mindset work everyday, you need to focus on <u>what</u> this entails. If you have the opportunity to see a psychiatrist or counselor, do it. Having a guided session with a professional who can help you identify blocks and work through all of them is always a bonus. If you don't have the ability to do so, there are plenty of opportunities to work on your mindset by yourself. Focus on the list I gave you earlier in the chapter and start incorporating those activities into your day-to-day life.

If you're a reader, I would start with Carol Dweck's book, Mindset. You should also pick up Overcoming Underearning by Barbara Stanny. The third book can either be You Are A Badass by Jen Sincere or The Subtle Art of Not Giving An F by Mark Manson.

If you're not a reader, I don't know why you're

still here and don't know what to tell you. You should probably talk to another non-reader, because I don't think you and I can be friends. There is just too much between us.

Alright, alright, we can still be friends, but I still don't know why you started reading my book if you're not even a reader in the first place. Although I'm flattered you chose to read mine.

Oh, it's because you like me? You like me?! You really do!

I'm so happy! I like you too! I hope you've enjoyed our time together and have learned some helpful stuff. We are almost at the point where we have to say goodbye, but let's enjoy the time we have left together.

KAYLEE WHITE

How Not to be Just Another Freelancer

Chapter Twenty-Five

IT'S AMAZING HOW FAR we can go and how much we can change in such a short time. When I first started this book, I had an idea of how it was going to go. By the end of it, my idea and the point of this book had completely changed. That was just the first draft. By the time I publish this book, it will have completely changed. That is the point though - experiences like reading someone else's story, learning new ways of thinking, and changing your beliefs are all vital to improving your business and your life.

This journey is far from over. Now, it's time to start implementing everything you've learned into your everyday practices. It's time to give yourself the opportunity to make every dream you've had come true. This isn't for the weak. This is going to take a lot of work. When people realize they could actually get everything they've ever hoped for, they panic. They start to self-sabotage their potential success by going after the wrong clients, focusing on the wrong things, and completely freezing and stopping all forward progress. This won't be you. You have a ton of resources at your fingertips. Don't panic.

Remember everything you've learned. Take time to celebrate your successes. Understand how things end up the way they do and learn from your mistakes. Do everything in your power to move forward. Keep a positive mindset and focus on what you do best. Reread this book if you ever get lost. You're here to be the best version of yourself in order to create the best life you can.

This is it. We're at the end now - I warned you this moment would come. It's as hard for me as it is for you. I want to keep this book in my hands longer, but the time has come for you to take this book and start changing the world.

You're more than ready to do this. You have the skills and know what you need to do. You're not just another freelancer.

You're a business owner.

KAYLEE WHITE

Thanks for reading! Please add a short review on Amazon and let me know what you thought!

Amazon reviews are extremely helpful for authors. Thank you for taking the time to support me and my work. Don't forget to share your review on social media with the hashtag #notjustanotherfreelancer and encourage others to read this book too!

KAYLEE WHITE

DON'T FORGET TO SIGN UP FOR THE MONTHLY NEWSLETTER

TO RECEIVE SPECIAL OFFERS, GIVEAWAYS, DISCOUNTS, BONUS CONTENT, UPDATES FROM THE AUTHOR, INFO ON NEW RELEASE AND MORE:

WWW.KAYLEEWRITES.COM

P.S. Our resource center password is hnaf19kw. You'll need it to access the free templates and guides there!

ACKNOWLEDGEMENTS

Thank you, Russell, for pushing me to do this. I wouldn't be where I am today in my writing career or in my life without you. Thank you for everything you do for me. I love you!

I learned everything from authors like Kristen Martin, Bethany Atazadeh, Sarra Cannon, and so many more. Thank you for being willing to share your wisdom, support, and enthusiasm.

A big thank you to my Critic Partner and cover designer, J.M. Ivie! You kept me excited and pumped about my book the whole time. Thank you!

A ginormous thank you to my family who are always willing to support me in anything I do! Thank you for always wanting to be involved in my life – even if you do drive me crazy. I appreciate everything you do for me.

And of course, a humongous thank you to all of my readers. Without you, my books wouldn't have a home. There's a lot more to come! Have a bright and colourful day!

KAYLEE WHITE

About the Author

Kaylee White is an Authortuber who helps writers understand and conquer the Business Side of Writing. She lives with her fiance, Russell, and her spoiled Beagle, Basset Hound, Ollie, in San Diego, CA. She writes nonfiction and YA.

CONNECT WITH KAYLEE:
Website: www.kayleewrites.com
YouTube: Kaylee Writes
Instagram: @kayleewrites
Twitter: @kayleewritescom
Facebook: @kayleewritescom

www.ingramcontent.com/pod-product-compliance
Lightning Source LLC
Chambersburg PA
CBHW031622210526
45464CB00004B/1701